SIX SECRETS
TO A
POWERFUL
QUIET TIME

D0110901

SIX SECRETS
TO A
POWERFUL
QUIET TIME

Catherine Martin

HARVEST HOUSE PUBLISHERS

EUGENE, OREGON

Published in association with the literary agency of WordServe Literary Group, Ltd., 10152 S. Knoll Circle, Highlands Ranch, CO 80130

The author has made every effort to locate the owners of copyrighted materials quoted in this book. Upon notification, the author will make proper corrections in subsequent printings.

Back cover author photo © Phil Córdova

Cover by Koechel Peterson & Associates, Inc., Minneapolis, Minnesota

SIX SECRETS TO A POWERFUL QUIET TIME
Copyright © 2005 by Catherine Martin
Published by Harvest House Publishers
Eugene, Oregon 97402
www.harvesthousepublishers.com

Library of Congress Cataloging-in-Publication Data

Martin, Catherine, M.A.
    [Radical intimacy]
    Six secrets to a powerful quiet time / Catherine Martin.
        p. cm.
    Includes bibliographical references.
    Originally published: Radical intimacy. Palm Desert, Calif. : Quiet Time Ministries, 2005.
    ISBN-13: 978-0-7369-1745-2 (pbk.)
    ISBN-10: 0-7369-1745-4
  1. Devotion.   2. Spiritual life—Christianity.   I. Title.
    BV4815.M35 2006
    248.4—dc22   2005019224

Printed in the United States of America

07 08 09 10 11 12 13 /VP-CF/ 10 9 8 7 6 5 4 3

Dedicated to
the Lord Jesus Christ,
who has given me
the opportunity and privilege of
radical intimacy,

To the members of my precious family,
who have taught me
so much about intimacy:
David G. Martin, MD
Elizabeth Stuter Snyder
Robert J. Snyder
Robert and Tania Snyder
Kayla and Christopher
Eloise Martin
Ann and Andy Martin
Keegan and James
Nana,

To all my beloved friends,
who have shared their hearts
with me in fellowship,

To the people on the Quiet Time team,
who have served tirelessly
side by side with me in ministry,

And to the women of Southwest Community Church,
who have taught me so much about love
and dedication to the Lord.

CONTENTS

FOREWORD

*I*n this amazing journey called life, people and events mark our path, and we have opportunities to mark the path of others. I have reached the stage in my life where I can reflect with joy on my influence in someone's life and then realize that the student I once influenced has now become my teacher. Catherine Martin is such a person. I recently finished her book *A Heart to See Forever* and was praying about my next study. I decided to telephone Catherine's office to request another study when she telephoned back asking me to write the foreword for *Six Secrets to a Powerful Quiet Time*. What a blessing this has turned out to be!

I am challenged by Catherine's words "radical" and "reckless." It is easy to interpret these words with a negative connotation. However, as I have thought about challenging people to become radical disciples of Jesus, I believe this connotes *a complete dedication to; above the ordinary; an attractive commitment to be desired.* "Reckless" introduces a tone of adventure and a willingness to risk everything without thought of self or cost, and it has no thought of what can be gained.

In a relationship with God, radical recklessness cannot be our own effort. It is a call and work of God in a person's life. It is a result of knowledge and understanding of God, of who He is and what He has done in redeeming us from eternal separation from Himself, and of heaven and all the delightful promises God has given to mankind. As Oswald Chambers makes so clear, as we become more intimately acquainted with Jesus, we become more separated to God for one purpose—to proclaim God's love and forgiveness offered through Jesus Christ. That is the radical recklessness I want in my life and which I believe God wants to perfect in the life of every believer. It is possible only as we live every moment of every day yielded to the Holy Spirit.

We have just passed the second anniversary of my beloved Bill's departure for heaven. These have been meaningful and important years despite my loss of Bill's physical presence. I have learned so much from my Lord. He is so real, so nurturing and comforting, and I have come to know Him in a more intimate way. I am reminded many times that God is taking good care of me.

I have been thinking recently that I should reevaluate my life verses and my personal statement of faith in light of my future living and ministering alone. This book is just what I needed to help in guiding my thoughts and giving me scriptural content to search my heart and God's heart for me.

Interestingly enough, Psalm 27:4 was a verse God gave me in 1978 when I was facing major surgery and my first experience in the hospital. As a result, I imagined myself crawling into the arms of Jesus and being carried by Him in a bubble through all of the apprehension, pain, and discomfort. The verse has been a comfort to me many times since. Now, Catherine has made it even more meaningful as she has shared the significance of this verse in her life.

Catherine makes an intimate relationship with Jesus so attractive and so reasonably attainable. Her encouragement for the reader to have a daily quiet time and her creative ways to make the best use of that time are delightful. Her shared habit of journaling is inspiring, and I will certainly now add it more regularly to my daily devotional routine.

Catherine's writing style and grasp of biblical and theological information is very impressive. She obviously lives what she teaches. I like her emphasis on being a radical disciple of Jesus Christ and attaining radical intimacy with Him. When Catherine attended a conference of more than 1000 students at Arrowhead Springs in 1977, the students were challenged to respond to a message from Isaiah 6. They were asked to stand and to say their name and the words, "Lord, I will go." She responded to an immediate call and presented her life to God without reservation.

What she did that day has been the response of thousands and thousands of students around the world. She adopted the words of Oswald Chambers, "to become a radical disciple of Jesus Christ and recklessly abandoned to the will of God." These words depict so much the attitude of staff and students of Campus Crusade for Christ. So much do they represent the heart of staff that when I read of her commitment, immediately I thought of a way to inscribe a plaque with those words in memorial to a dear friend.

When you visit the Campus Crusade for Christ Headquarters at Lake Hart in Orlando, you will see a plaque placed in each of the elevators of our administrative buildings. Such is the commitment of my own life, and I challenge every believer to make that kind of a commitment in seeking "a radical, intimate relationship with God." My quiet time will be all the more enriched as a result of reading and applying Catherine's teaching in this book. Regardless of where you are in your Christian walk, you will enjoy this study. May God richly bless your quiet time as He has mine.

Vonette Z. Bright

You will seek Me and find Me
when you search for Me with all your heart.

JEREMIAH 29:13

INTRODUCTION

Six Secrets to a Powerful Quiet Time arose from my insatiable desire for a deeper devotional life with God—for radical intimacy with Him. In 1978 I created a personal notebook with journal, prayer, and Bible study pages. Over the years, one God-given idea has led to another. The results include the quiet time plan—P.R.A.Y.E.R.—introduced through Quiet Time Ministries in 1993, and *The Quiet Time Notebook,* published by Quiet Time Ministries since 1994. The first complete book of quiet times, *Pilgrimage of the Heart,* grew out of others' need to experience quiet time for themselves. NavPress published *Pilgrimage of the Heart, Revive My Heart!,* and *A Heart That Dances* in 2003. Quiet Time Ministries expanded the Quiet Times for the Heart series with *A Heart on Fire* and *A Heart to See Forever* in 2003–2004. *Six Secrets to a Powerful Quiet Time: Discovering Radical Intimacy with God* is the journey that will take you from an acquaintance with God to deep, intimate fellowship with Him. It answers the question, how do I really have a quiet time?

HOW TO USE *Six Secrets to a Powerful Quiet Time*

Each week you will *read, respond,* and *experience:*

- *Read*—As you read through each day's material on this journey of discovering radical intimacy with God, interact with the ideas by underlining what is significant to you and writing your comments in the margins. This book will encourage you to learn, grow, and develop a rich inner life with God. Please mark it up and make it yours!

- *Respond*—To help you think through and apply all that is written here, I have included a devotional response section at the end of each day: *Date, Key Verse, For Further Thought,* and *Response.* The key verse is included for you to meditate on and even memorize. For further thought, you will find questions to think about. Next you will find a place for you to express your thoughts and respond to what you have read. This is your opportunity to dialogue with God about radical intimacy and drawing near to Him.

- *Experience*—For practical application, use the complete quiet time at the end of every week, which emphasizes the principles included in that section. You can use the blank Notes page at the end of each week to record what you learn from the *Six Secrets* DVD (see page 272).

- *Share your journey*—Read what others are learning on their journey of discovering radical intimacy with God at www.quiettime.org. Share your own insights with others throughout the world, posting your thoughts on the message board.

SUGGESTED APPROACHES FOR *Six Secrets*
TO A POWERFUL QUIET TIME

You can benefit from this book in several ways:

- *Sequential*—You may want to read the book a day at a time and implement the principles before moving to the next chapter.

- *Topical*—You may have specific topics of interest to you. If that is the case, then you may look at the table of contents and focus on those topics.

- *Devotional*—You may choose to read this book in 30 days. The days are divided into five sections so that you can take five weeks to read and think about your quiet time. It can be a 30-day adventure.

SUGGESTED SETTINGS FOR *SIX SECRETS TO A POWERFUL QUIET TIME*

- *Personal and private*—Six Secrets to a Powerful Quiet Time is the kind of book you can read again and again. It will encourage you to draw near to God, especially if you are in a season where you have lost the habit of spending time with your Lord or if you need to shake up your quiet time because it has become lackluster and routine. You might even want to spend some extended time with this book in a beautiful setting to revive and refresh your relationship with the Lord—a retreat in a book!

- *Small groups*—I encourage you to travel on this quiet time journey with some friends. What a joy it is to share what you are learning with others who also love the Lord. You may use the questions at the end of each day for your discussion together or use the questions in appendix 1. Six accompanying messages on DVD are available from Quiet Time Ministries (Introductory week through week 5—see page 271). This book may be used in Sunday school classes, Bible study groups, church congregations, or in your family devotions.

- *Ministry revival campaign*—You may also desire to use this book as a 30-day intensive campaign to teach, revive, and inspire those in your ministry. This is a great way to prepare for a yearlong Bible study. In addition, using it as a campaign will help grow your ministry as you form new small groups.

In order to organize your quiet time, you may want to experience *The Quiet Time Notebook*, published by Quiet Time Ministries Press. In addition, *A Heart That Dances*, published by NavPress in 2003, is a complete book of quiet times devoted to the subject of intimacy with God. It's a perfect companion to *Six Secrets to a Powerful Quiet Time* (see Quiet Time Ministries Resources at www.quiettime.org for a complete description of all the books in the Quiet Times for the Heart series).

Enough preparation—let's begin the journey! I would not have you simply watch a travelogue on the Holy Land. I would rather you touch for yourself the blades of grass on the Mount of Olives and watch the sun glisten on the Sea of Galilee. We are about to embark on a journey of the pursuit of God, where you'll experience the real excitement of knowing Him. My prayer is that you will taste and see that the Lord is good. May God richly bless you on this journey.

Week One

THE GREAT ADVENTURE

❧

Days 1-6

THE INVITATION TO RADICAL INTIMACY

I have loved you with an everlasting love.

JEREMIAH 31:3

God wants you—not a part of you but all of you, every day and all the time. When you open your mind to this truth and surrender to it, your devotion to God will begin to deepen. There is no one He would rather spend time with than you. He says, "I have loved you with an everlasting love" (Jeremiah 31:3). God desires something astounding with you: *radical intimacy.*

When we think of intimacy, we usually think of marriage. Intimacy with God is much deeper than surface acquaintance, and it is marked by friendship and emotional closeness. It is private and personal, with love, warmth, and intense joy. Intimacy with God is real, revolutionary, radical, and relational.

- It's real because it's not theoretical but a true experience.

- It's revolutionary because knowing Him intimately will transform your life.

- It's radical because as it changes your life, your intimate relationship with God will have an impact on the world.

- It's relational, implying an exchange and interaction with the Creator of the universe.

Radical intimacy with God is a deep, abiding sharing of hearts no outward circumstance can touch. There is a mutuality in your relationship with the Lord; it is not one-sided. Scripture confirms this as we see God constantly initiating relationships with men and women such as Abraham, Moses, Hagar, and David. When we cry out to God, an amazing thing happens. He responds to our prayers. When King Hezekiah was threatened by an enemy, he took his trouble to the Lord. God responded by rescuing him from impending danger. Scripture corroborates over and over again that radical intimacy is not merely perfunctory but something God invites you to enjoy—a pleasure. However, it takes time. It grows through experience and engagement with God.

At the heart of your relationship with the Lord is time with Him— quiet time. Quiet time with God every day is initiated by God, led by God, and enriched by God. He has provided everything necessary for intimacy: the Word of God, prayer, the indwelling Holy Spirit, the companionship of Jesus, and the fellowship of good friends. All the men and women who have gone anywhere with the Lord have always cultivated time alone with Him in His Word and in prayer. This is the most important part of your day. Lots of people talk about spending time with God; very few actually do it. Rarely will this practice be encouraged in church. That may sound like a harsh commentary of our day and time, but how else can we account for the fact that only 45 percent of church attendees open their Bibles outside of church?[1] Rarely do people in church talk about what they learned in their quiet time. Rarely do pastors speak of their time with God. There is sermon preparation, hospital visitation, and ministry organization, but where is the presence of God? Has God left the church? No. I would venture to say that the church has, in a fashion, stepped away from God. This is not a new thing. People have been neglecting their own personal relationships with God since the beginning of time. Even in the garden of Eden, Adam hid from God after eating the forbidden fruit rather than showing up for their daily walk in the garden.

I remember sharing a devotion in seminary on the subject of quiet time. When I sat down, another student stood up in front of the class to give the next devotion. He said, "I don't think I have ever understood what it means to have a quiet time." Then the next classmate gave his devotion. As an introduction, he said, "I've never had a quiet time like that before." I was so surprised by their words. A friend leaned over and whispered to me, "Most of these guys don't know anything about spending time with God." These were people who were studying to be pastors and full-time workers in Christian ministry, and yet they knew very little about time with God.

People often acquire academic facts about God without a real, vital interaction or experience with Him. Yet God desires a dynamic, authentic relationship with us. God said to the people of Israel, "Here am I, Here am I...I have spread out My hands all day long to a rebellious people" (Isaiah 65:1-2). What He seemed to be saying to them was, "Where are you? I want you with Me. I want to share life with you. I have much to give you. I want you to know Me."

Jesus said, "Behold, I stand at the door and knock; if anyone hears My voice and opens the door, I will come in to him and will dine with him, and he with Me" (Revelation 3:20). Oh, what a picture this paints for the people of God! Jesus wants to sit down at the dinner table and talk with you over a good meal. His words point to intimate conversation and a sharing of thoughts and ideas. They also imply radical impact and transformation. Can you imagine the difference in your life if you spend time every day with Jesus? You will never be the same.

God is extending an invitation to you to be intimate with Him. To know Him. To walk with Him. It is an invitation to radical intimacy. It is written all across the pages of His Word.

- In Psalm 46:10 (NIV) God says, "Be still, and know that I am God."

- In Jeremiah 9:23-24 He says, "Let not a wise man boast of his wisdom, and let not the mighty man boast of his might, let not a rich man boast of his riches; but let him who boasts boast of this, that he understands and knows Me, that I am the LORD who exercises lovingkindness, justice, and righteousness on earth; for I delight in these things."

- In Matthew 11:28 Jesus says, "Come to Me, all you who are weary and heavy-laden, and I will give you rest."

- In John 7:37 Jesus says, "If anyone is thirsty, let him come to Me and drink."

- In Revelation 3:20 Jesus says, "Behold, I stand at the door and knock; if anyone hears My voice and opens the door, I will come in to him, and will dine with him, and he with Me."

The Hebrew word for "know" in Jeremiah 9:23-24 is *yada* and implies an actual experience with God, not an academic acquiring of facts. He wants you to know Him in your everyday experience of life. Day by day, in your quiet time with God, you will learn about His attributes, His love, His power, His wisdom, His peace, His sovereignty, and more. You will understand the magnificence of His ways and purposes. As you learn these truths, you will trust Him to work in your life. You will talk with Him moment by moment. With time, you will begin to recognize His presence and power in your own life. This firsthand experience with God is incomparable, and once you have enjoyed His presence, nothing else will come close to satisfying the needs of your heart and soul.

Remember, God is the One extending this invitation to intimacy. That is important. It is not just an acquaintance extending an invitation to meet with you. It is not your neighbor. It is not the pastor of your church. It is not even the president of the United States. It is God Himself, the Creator and CEO of the universe, the King of kings and the Lord of lords.

Men and women whose lives are displayed in the Word of God understood the delight and priority of intimacy with God.

- Moses said to God, "Let me know Your ways that I may know You, so that I may find favor in Your sight" (Exodus 33:13).

- David, the man after God's own heart, said, "Make me know Your ways, O LORD; Teach me Your paths" (Psalm 25:4).

- Hosea said, "Come, let us return to the LORD...So let us know, let us press on to know the LORD" (Hosea 6:1,3).

- Paul said, "I count all things to be loss in view of the surpassing value of knowing Christ Jesus my Lord" (Philippians 3:8).

The exciting part about quiet time is that the Lord's invitation is a winning proposition. Why? Because God wants to be intimate with you—radically intimate. David knew this very well. He said, "Friendship with the LORD is reserved for those who fear him. With them he shares the secrets of his covenant" (Psalm 25:14 NLT). Only intimates share secrets. And God desires to share His secrets with you.

Think about Zaccheus. He wanted to see Jesus in person, but some obstacles made this desire seemingly impossible. He was a chief tax collector with a lot of responsibility and power—time was precious. He was rich, and Jesus seemed to spend time with those who were poor. Then too, Zaccheus was small in stature and struggled to catch a glimpse of Jesus in a large crowd. But he wanted to see Jesus so much that he became creative. He ran ahead of the crowd, climbed up a sycamore tree, and waited eagerly. Jesus walked right under the tree where Zaccheus was perched, looked up, and said to him, "Zaccheus, hurry and come down, for today I must stay at your house" (Luke 19:5). What would you do if Jesus walked into the room where you are right now, looked into your eyes, and said, "Today I would like to spend quiet time with you"? Here's what Zaccheus did. He hurried down and received Him with great joy. Will you do the same?

What does God's invitation to radical intimacy really mean for you in your own life?

- God invites you to a pilgrimage of the heart (Psalm 84:5), to find your home in God while journeying in a foreign land until you reach your grand destination: heaven.

- God invites you to personal, spiritual revival (John 7:37-38), to constant renewal, and to a restoration of God's purpose and plan for your life.

- God invites you to share His heart (Psalm 46:10), to move in perfect step with Him as He leads you through life, and to enjoy intimate fellowship with Him.

- God invites you to influence the world (Luke 24:32) with a heart burning with a contagious love that spreads to those around you.

- God invites you to an eternal perspective (2 Corinthians 4:18), seeing life from God's point of view, looking beyond the temporal to the eternal.

- God invites you to radical discipleship (Matthew 4:19), paying the price in time and energy to sit at His feet and learn from Him.

(These thoughts are developed more fully in my books of quiet times: *Pilgrimage of the Heart, Revive My Heart!, A Heart That Dances, A Heart on Fire,* and *A Heart to See Forever.*)

At the outset of your journey into quiet time with the Lord, you must make a decision. Will you be that rare person who, with a longing heart, will open the pages of your Bible, day by day, to hear and respond to what God has to say? Will you be radical for Him and say yes to this invitation to engage in radical intimacy? If so, write a prayer of commitment to the Lord in the space provided under "My Response" on page 26. This does not mean that you will never again miss a day of time with the Lord. It means that your heart's desire is to know the Lord, and you will endeavor to set aside time with Him and pay the price in time and energy to know Him. It is a commitment to intentional devotion.

These pages contain something of my own passion and pursuit of God. This is a sharing of ideas, a guide into the presence of the Lord—how to get there and what to do when you meet together with Him. Imagine that we are fellow pilgrims, climbing the great mountain of God. We are going to sit together on the mountaintop for a while, savor the vast expanse of God, and talk about practical ways to draw near to Him. We will think together about many things: What is this radical intimacy? What makes it surpass a simple devotional life? How can you achieve it? Once you do, how will you keep it going? What should you do to have a deeper knowledge of God? If desire is necessary, where do you get the desire? The very fact that you are reading this book is proof that you are already on the journey. But there is much to discover. And God will guide you. Developing a deep devotion to God is not a passive process. You cannot experience God through osmosis. This book contains time-tested disciplines of devotion. Experiment with them, experience the adventure of knowing God, and enjoy the journey along the way.

My Response

DATE:

KEY VERSE: "Be still, and know that I am God" (Psalm 46:10 NIV).

FOR FURTHER THOUGHT: Will you write a letter to the Lord in response to His invitation to radical intimacy? Include your own dreams and desires for your relationship with Him. If you have never established a relationship with God and desire to know Him, will you pray to Him now and invite Jesus Christ into your life? If this is the desire of your heart, you may pray the following prayer: *Lord Jesus, I need You. I invite You now to come into my life, forgive my sins, and make me the person You want me to be. In Jesus' name. Amen.*

MY RESPONSE: *A Letter to the Lord*

THE PATH TO RADICAL INTIMACY

Clearly, you are a letter from Christ.

2 CORINTHIANS 3:3 NLT

⁓∽

od has a message to write on your heart. When your heart dances with the Lord, the dance tells a story to the world. It's the story of your life with Him. That's why knowing God is such an adventure. Paul said to the Corinthian church, "Clearly, you are a letter from Christ" (2 Corinthians 3:3). What message does God want to write on the tablet of your heart for the world to see?

When I was young, the concept of quiet time was an intriguing mystery to me. I longed to interact with God and experience Him in a real and tangible way. My first quiet time adventure with God began when I was a junior in high school. On a warm summer weekend, I set out on a trip to Oak Creek Canyon in Arizona, an area enveloped by Sedona's red rock mountains. Even at this tender age I felt a deeper yearning toward God. I knew I wanted to know Him, but I did not know how. So one day, I got up early, tucked my Bible in my backpack, and began hiking up an immense mountain. It took me more than an hour to get to the top, but I was richly rewarded for my efforts.

On top of the mountain I discovered a beautiful meadow painted with wildflowers and framed by lush green pine trees. Beyond the meadow, I saw a breathtaking view of Oak Creek Canyon spreading out before me. The red rocks, with all their varying shapes, jutted upward in a geometric symphony that could only point to a magnificent Creator. At that moment, I was filled with a sense of awe at the majesty of God. I must know Him!

Sitting down, I opened my Bible and began reading the Sermon on the Mount in Matthew 5–7. "Blessed are the poor in spirit, for theirs is the kingdom of heaven. Blessed are those who mourn, for they shall be comforted. Blessed are the gentle, for they shall inherit the earth. Blessed are those who hunger and thirst for righteousness, for they shall be satisfied…" As I read those words, I sensed the Lord was inviting me to a life that I did not yet know, a life I desired at a deep and intense level in my own heart. It was "life on the highest plane," as Ruth Paxson described many years ago in a book by the same title—a life of purity and holiness, blessing and adventure, rest and communion. In essence, intimacy with God. Now I very much wanted this kind of life, but I could see that it would require something of me. This life would be freely given, but I knew I would have to respond to God's invitation to join Him with a decision of commitment and reckless abandonment. I committed myself to become way beyond who I was at the moment—a radical choice for a young girl. I got out a piece of paper and wrote a simple prayer to the Lord:

> Lord, I give myself to You. I want to live for You in this world. I want to know You. I want the kind of life described in the Bible. I don't know what it will mean, but I know I desire You more than anything else. I give up all my own dreams and goals to grasp Your plan for my life. In Jesus' name. Amen.

I folded that paper and buried it on top of that mountain as a promise to God and to myself. That piece of paper in Sedona has disintegrated with time. However, I believe that the Lord has not forgotten that prayer, nor have I. That commitment was just the beginning of the most exciting adventure in all of life: the great adventure of knowing God. It is what I describe as radical intimacy. Why radical? Because of the depth of relationship that is possible with God in our everyday life and the commitment required from us to experience it. God says: "You will seek Me and find Me when you search for Me with all your heart" (Jeremiah 29:13). Radical intimacy is dangerous because you are opening your heart to God. It is the part of you that can be touched and moved and changed. This deep intimacy requires a sacrifice in time and energy, but knowing God this way is worth infinitely more than great wealth and possessions. Radical intimacy is worth every minute of fervent prayer, every hour of intense study, and every day of sweet surrender to God amid the trials of life.

That day I sat on top of that mountain and wrote my prayer of commitment to the Lord was not the last time I would express my desire to follow Christ. If Jesus really was the way, the truth, and the life, then to live for anything else was to live for a lie. Soon I became involved with Campus Crusade for Christ at Arizona State University, where I was discipled by Leann Pruitt McGee, a Campus Crusade for Christ staff member. I would open my Bible one day, but then I might not open it for many days thereafter. Then one day, in a quiet time, I read Psalm 27:4, which David wrote during one of the most difficult times of his life: "One thing I have asked from the LORD, that I shall seek: That I may dwell in the house of the LORD all the days of my life, to behold the beauty of the LORD, and to meditate in His temple." In this verse I clearly understood that the Lord longed for me to be intimate with Him. He wanted to be that one great thing in my life.

Walt Henrichsen's little book says it all with the probing title, *Many Aspire, Few Attain*. Do you aspire to be intimate with the Lord? If so, how can you attain such a radical goal? The answer is much time spent alone with God—quiet time. Quiet time flows from your commitment to pursue God. Commitment requires follow-through. And follow-through requires dedication. And dedication comes directly from the knowledge of God.

J.I. Packer says in *Knowing God*, "What, of all the states God ever sees man in, gives God most pleasure? Knowledge of Himself."[1] But A.W. Tozer in *The Pursuit of God* asks the salient question: "Why do some persons find God in a way that others do not?" Then he gives the answer: "I venture to suggest that the one vital quality that they had in common was spiritual receptivity...They acquired the lifelong habit of spiritual response."[2] Tozer helped me understand more clearly that many Christians will not pay the price in time and energy to be intimate with the Lord. How sad but true. C.S. Lewis has said that the problem is not that our desires are too strong but that they are too weak. To know God is to understand the purpose of life, to comprehend the meaning of our own existence, to find help in time of need, and to grasp God's eternal perspective in all things.

This journey of quiet time with the Lord has led to many adventures in my own ministry: on staff with Campus Crusade for Christ and the Josh McDowell Ministry, a graduate of Bethel Theological Seminary, the Director of Women's Ministries at a large church in southern California, an adjunct professor at Biola University, and the president of Quiet Time Ministries. Out of my quiet times have come numerous books, retreats, conferences, a training center, and opportunities I could never have dreamed of when I was in college. God gave me the ideas, the strength, and the wisdom to carry out those ideas. How powerful and true are these words I heard from Ney Bailey of Campus Crusade for Christ: You be responsible for the depth of ministry and go deep with God, and let God be responsible for the breadth of your ministry.

What I have shared with you is my story, my own personal adventure of knowing God through quiet time with Him. But the Lord has a message to write on your heart and a story of your life to tell. Drawing near to God and spending time with Him is not an option—it's a necessity. It's not legalism but love. Love for Jesus Christ. As we spend time with Jesus, our love grows, and we will crave time alone with Him the way a lover longs for her beloved's presence. Will you say yes to His invitation of intimacy? "The eyes of the LORD move to and fro throughout the earth that He may strongly support those whose heart is completely His" (2 Chronicles 16:9). May His eyes rest on you and on me.

My Response

DATE:

KEY VERSE: "Thus says the LORD, 'Let not a wise man boast of his wisdom, and let not the mighty man boast of his might, let not a rich man boast of his riches; but let him who boasts boast of this, that he understands and knows Me, that I am the LORD who exercises lovingkindness, justice and righteousness on earth; for I delight in these things,' declares the LORD" (Jeremiah 9:23-24).

FOR FURTHER THOUGHT: Where are you in the great adventure of knowing God? What is the story of your life with Him? How has your heart danced with the Lord?

MY RESPONSE:

Day Three

THE GOAL OF RADICAL INTIMACY

Run in such a way that you may win.

I CORINTHIANS 9:24

ocusing on your goal will take you to your destination. Paul encourages us to "run in such a way that you may win" (1 Corinthians 9:24). The question is, how do we run toward this goal of radical intimacy?

One day, a man was driving a horse-drawn taxi in Dublin. His occupant was Thomas Henry Huxley, a devoted disciple of Darwin. Mr. Huxley was in a hurry to catch his train to the next city. He assumed that the driver of the taxi had been told the destination by the hotel doorman, so all he said when he got in was, "Hurry, I'm almost late. Drive fast!" The horses lurched forward and galloped at a vigorous pace. Before long Huxley glanced out the window and frowned as he realized they were going west, away from the sun, not toward it. The scholar shouted, "Do you know where you are going?" Without looking back, the driver yelled back, "No, your honor, but I'm driving very fast." Many people live like that—running nowhere but doing it at a rapid pace.

Focus on the Goal

At the outset of the journey in quiet time, you must set your sights on the goal. Your goal? To know a Person—the Lord Jesus Christ. Everything in your life revolves around Him. God says, "Be still, and know that I am God" (Psalm 46:10 NIV). The construction of the Hebrew phrase implies that you stop everything, turn to God, and experience His reality and presence in your life. But radical intimacy requires the art of focus as well. You want to fix your eyes on Jesus. The writer of Hebrews says, "Let us also lay aside every encumbrance and the sin which so easily entangles us, and let us run with endurance the race that is set before us, fixing our eyes on Jesus, the author and perfecter of faith" (Hebrews 12:1-2). Focus on your goal just as a mariner traveling on the sea would keep his eyes on the lighthouse. Focusing on your goal will help you fix your position, avoid the rocks and cliffs, and stay on the road to intimacy with God.

A Life Verse and a Life Goal

One way to understand God's unique goal for you is to ask Him to give you a life verse that you can call your own. To begin, write out the verses that have been significant to you over the years. God may have already given you a verse that is your life focus. If not, ask Him to make one verse stand out, a verse that touches your heart and seems to inspire your own dreams and desires. Your life goal should be big enough to capture your heart for a lifetime. It should be based on and formed from the Word of God. It should be what you come back to at different stages of your life for guidance and direction. No loss, no trial, no difficult relationship can touch that one thing that is your ultimate goal from the Lord. (See appendix 2: "A Quiet Time for Determining Your Life Goal and Life Verse.")

David, the man after God's own heart, wrote his life goal in Psalm 27:4: "One thing I have asked from the Lord, that I shall seek: That I may dwell in the house of the LORD all the days of my life, to behold the beauty of the LORD and to meditate in His temple." In those days the temple represented the presence of the Lord. What David was saying is that more than anything he wanted intimacy with the Lord, both for himself and the people of Israel. That one goal influenced everything he did in his life. As a result, he established the public worship of God during his reign as king of Israel.

Your life goal and your life verse may differ from David's. The Lord may direct you in ways you may not yet be able to fathom. For J. Hudson Taylor, it meant going to China. For Billy Graham, it meant evangelistic crusades instead of going to seminary. For Bill Bright, it meant establishing the worldwide ministry of Campus Crusade for Christ to spread the gospel of Jesus Christ. For Jim Elliot, it meant the dream of taking the gospel to an unreached people, the Auca Indians. For Susannah Wesley, it meant praying in the middle of her kitchen with her apron over her head because that was the only time she could find with the Lord since he had called her to raise so many children. One woman's pursuit of God led her to put a sign above her kitchen sink that read "Divine service performed here three times a day." Because of her life goal, Hannah Whitall Smith stayed married to a man who had deep emotional problems and wandered away from faith in the Lord. Pursuit of God inspired Fanny Crosby to write more than 8000 hymns even though she was blind from early childhood.

Having a life goal and a life verse from the Lord will build in you a steadfastness that overcomes all obstacles in life. The one thing that will keep you from your pilgrimage with the Lord is to give up. Florence Chadwick, the first woman to swim the English Channel in both directions, set as her goal to swim from the California coast to Catalina Island. After 15 hours in freezing water, enveloped by fog and surrounded by sharks, she became discouraged and collapsed in a rescue boat with exhaustion. Although she had been swimming for more than 25 miles, she quit because the end was not in sight. Do you know how far she was from her goal? One-half mile. It is always too soon to give up. Focusing on your life goal and verse and then cultivating your pursuit of God by spending time with Him will keep you from quitting when life's waves get rough and the shoreline is not visible.

Benefits of Pursuing the Goal

What are the benefits of this pursuit to know God?

- Your actions and behavior in life will be characterized by wisdom (James 1:5).

- You will find that you have a place of refuge, a shelter in the storms of life (Psalm 46).

- You will experience a peace, a contentment, and a satisfaction that is independent of feelings or circumstances (Philippians 4:11-13).

- You will know God as the living God (1 Samuel 17:26-37).

- You will begin to look at events and people through God's eyes and from His perspective (2 Corinthians 4:17-18).

- You will have a sense of purpose, meaning, and direction in life as God works in and through you to change the world (Romans 12:1-2).

- You will appreciate the "you" God has designed (Acts 17:28).

- You will be renewed and receive life for a new day (John 7:37-38).

- You will find rest for your soul (Matthew 11:28-30).

- You will experience a peace that enables you to endure the difficulties of life (Philippians 4:6-7).

- You will experience clarity in the circumstances of your life (1 Corinthians 2:14-16).

- You will see and experience the kingdom of God (Matthew 6:33).

- You will gain strength to say no to sin, and you will experience a life of holiness (1 Peter 1:14-16).

- You will shine with the light of Jesus in the world (Matthew 5:14-16).

- You will apply the benefits of God's promises to your life (2 Peter 1:2-8).

- You will find that the joy of the Lord is your strength (Nehemiah 8:10; John 15:11).

- You will become a man or a woman after God's own heart (Acts 13:22).

What an adventure walking with the Lord is! It is what life is all about. Corrie Ten Boom used to call the life of faith a Fantastic Adventure In Trusting Him. She experienced the horrors of Ravensbruck concentration camp during World War II. And yet she was able to revel in the great adventure of knowing God at the same time. She taught many prisoners about God while in prison. She had a Bible, and for her, the words of God became precious, more precious than gold or silver. You see, the Nazis could not take the Lord from Corrie. They could take her father, her sister, her freedom. But they could not touch her relationship with the Lord. And so it is with you.

My Response

DATE:

KEY VERSE: "One thing I have asked from the LORD, that I shall seek: That I may dwell in the house of the LORD all the days of my life, to behold the beauty of the LORD, and to meditate in His temple" (Psalm 27:4).

FOR FURTHER THOUGHT: Will you take some time now and ask God to give you a life verse and a life goal that is great enough to capture your heart for a lifetime? You may wish to use the quiet time for determining your life goal and life verse in appendix 2 to help you think and pray about these things. If you know your life verse and life goal, will you write it out in the space provided?

MY RESPONSE:

THE QUIET TIME PLAN: WHERE DO I BEGIN?

Times of refreshing may come
from the presence of the Lord.

ACTS 3:19

ime with God is the most important part of your day. In Acts we see that "times of refreshing may come from the presence of the Lord" (Acts 3:19). No time is wasted that is spent with the Lord. This time determines every other activity in your life. It shapes your character. It influences your world: your family, your friends, your church, your ministry. Quiet time is vital for your spiritual growth.

One of the most common questions I receive about quiet time is "Where do I begin?" Jesus is our example. Taking periodic breaks to fellowship with His Father was the habit of His life. Luke tells us that "the news about Him was spreading even farther, and large crowds were gathering to hear Him and to be healed of their sicknesses. But Jesus Himself would often slip away to the wilderness and pray" (Luke 5:15-16). In these statements from Luke we see that Jesus led a busy life and was in great demand. Large crowds would seek Him out. To be alone was almost out of the question. What did Jesus do? He would "slip away to the wilderness and pray." Luke tells us that He did it often. That means it was a habit. He intentionally set aside a time in advance and purposely made a plan to do it. He went to the wilderness. He purposely chose a certain place that would be conducive to His time with His Father. And then He prayed. As you begin this great climb to know your God, it will help to set aside a time, a place, and a plan to be with Him each day. This sets the stage for all the magnificent things that happen in time alone with the Lord.

THE QUIET TIME

One of the first things that I learned in developing a quiet time with the Lord was that it involved intentional devotion. Quiet time is not something that just happens. It requires planning and preparation. If the president of the United States called you and invited you to lunch, you would not say, "Maybe I will, maybe I won't." You would say, "What time and where?" Think about it this way. The Lord, who is the CEO of the universe, desires time with you each day. We cannot say, "Maybe I will and maybe I won't." The response is, "What time and where?" Ask the Lord to help you determine the time. After all, God created you for fellowship with Him. He will make a way. Remember, the goal is *radical intimacy* with the Lord. Radical intimacy implies *radical choices* for the Lord against many good things that would keep us from being alone with Him. God will honor the sacrifice in time, energy, and sometimes even sleep to be alone with Him.

When is the best time to spend with the Lord? The Bible seems to emphasize the importance of the morning (Mark 1:35). David said in Psalm 5:3, "In the morning, O LORD, You will hear my voice; in the morning I will order my prayer to You and eagerly watch." In the morning Jacob made a vow to the Lord and set up a stone on the ground as a memorial to the Lord (Genesis 28:18). Moses made one of the grandest prayer requests when he said, "Lord, show me your glory" (see Exodus 33:18). God answered Moses' request in the morning when "the LORD descended in the cloud and stood there with him as he called upon the name of the LORD" (Exodus 34:5). Probably the greatest encouragement of all for quiet time in the morning is seen in the life of Jesus Himself. "In the early morning, while it was still dark, Jesus got up, left the house, and went away to a secluded place, and was praying there" (Mark 1:35).

The time you choose should be when you are most alert and you can be completely alone with the Lord. Sometimes, quiet time in the morning is absolutely impossible. For you, it may be midday or at night. Quiet time is a time when you withdraw from the activities and distractions of the world to sit alone with the Lord in His Word and in prayer.

Finding a time with the Lord will involve creativity and resourcefulness. It will also mean a certain ruthlessness that says no to other things in order to say yes to the Lord. You are going to learn the art of "slipping away" that Jesus practiced during His stay on earth (Luke 5:15-16). M. Basil Pennington says in his book *A Place Apart,* "What person can dare say they cannot afford to take time for apartness—indeed, who can afford not to take time for apartness?…There is in the lives of most of us a good bit more freedom and flexibility to organize such a dimension, *if we really want to.*" [1] Ask the Lord to show you the best time.

I remember one young mother who was so excited about beginning to spend time with the Lord. She got up early, brewed her coffee, and gathered her quiet time materials. Then, she sat down to have quiet time with the Lord. Within minutes, she heard the footsteps of her young children coming down the hall to join her. Did she give up? No. This creative mother decided to help her young children establish their own quiet times. She explained that she was having quiet time with the Lord. She helped them each sit down and be alone with the Lord. Soon, those little ones could not wait to get up early and have a quiet time just like their mother. Another lady came up to me and said there was absolutely not one moment in the day that she could spend time with the Lord. I suggested she ask the Lord to find a time for her. Later, she came up to me and excitedly shared how God had shown her that she could draw near to Him during her lunch hour.

People often ask me how much time I spend with the Lord. I answer, sometimes ten minutes and sometimes two hours. It all depends how much time I have and how much time I am willing to set aside to know the Lord. My quiet time is usually about an hour. But sometimes the Lord takes me on a journey in His Word, and then I tarry even longer with Him. Like all relationships of friendship and intimacy, our times together vary in length and intensity. But if we miss these bonding moments or rush too many of our times together, we miss a richness and depth of love. Connecting on an intimate level is the goal. A.W. Tozer wrote in his first editorial for *Alliance Weekly*, dated June 3, 1950, "It will cost something to walk slow in the parade of the ages while excited men of time rush about confusing motion with progress. But it will pay in the long run and the true Christian is not much interested in anything short of that."

THE QUIET PLACE

Radical intimacy flourishes in a quiet place. God says, "In quietness and trust is your strength" (Isaiah 30:15). Have you found your quiet "place" with the Lord?

It is clear that Jesus was the master of the art of finding the quiet place (Luke 5:15-16). When He wanted to commune with His Father and spend time with intimate friends, He would travel to Bethany, two miles from Jerusalem on the far side of the Mount of Olives, out in the country, covered with fruit trees and waving grain. Jesus probably walked to Bethany after busy days in Jerusalem, savoring the journey with His Father. His friends often observed Him amid the trees or the grassy fields in deep communion with God the Father.

Everyone needs a Bethany. Jesus invites you to "Come with me by yourselves to a quiet place and get some rest" (Mark 6:31 NIV). Henri Nouwen says that "we have, indeed, to fashion our own desert where we can withdraw every day, shake off our compulsions, and dwell in the gentle healing presence of our Lord."[2]

Robert Murray McCheyne, a pastor at St. Peter's Church in Dundee, Scotland, in the early 1800s, embarked on a rigorous ministry trip through Europe. McCheyne and his fellow travelers encountered a raging storm on the Mediterranean Sea and were forced to land on a desert island. Listen to what McCheyne said about this event in the letter to his church contained in the *Memoirs and Remains of Robert Murray McCheyne* by Andrew Bonar:

> I thought that perhaps this providence was given me that I might have a quiet day to pray for you. There were about twelve fishermen's huts on the island, made of reeds, with a vine growing before the door, and a fig tree in their garden. We gave tracts and books in French to all our fellow passengers, and to the inhabitants, and tried to hallow the Sabbath. My heart went up to God the whole day for you all, and for my dear friends who would be ministering to you. I tried to go over you one by one, as many as I could call to mind. My longing desire for you was, that Jesus might reveal Himself to you in the breaking of bread, that you might have heart-filling views of the lovely person of Immanuel, and might draw from Him rivers of comfort, life, and holiness.[3]

That remote island became a sanctuary for McCheyne. With God there, it was holy ground—McCheyne's quiet place.

When do you need this quiet place? Every day, especially in challenging life situations. You need to "come away" *when you get troubling news.* When Jesus heard the news about the death of John the Baptist, He left in a boat to find a quiet place alone (Matthew 14:13). You need a quiet place *in a time of popularity and success.* One time a whole city gathered at the door where Jesus was staying. What did Jesus do? He got up early in the morning and went to a deserted place and prayed there (Mark 1:35). You need a quiet place *after a time of intense ministry.* After the disciples came back from their ministry adventure of preaching and teaching, the Lord invited them to come away with Him and rest awhile (Mark 6:31-32). Finally, you need a quiet place *when there are huge demands on you and you have little time to yourself.* Jesus was constantly surrounded by people. What would He do? He would leave the place where He was staying and find a quiet place (Luke 5:15-16).

A.W. Tozer, pastor of Chicago's Southside Alliance church and editor of *Alliance Weekly*, was a man who enjoyed great popularity in his ministry, and yet he was known as one who spent much time in his office with his door closed, alone with God. One biographer noted that Tozer spent more time on his knees than at his desk. Another person noted that "this man makes you want to know and feel God." Tozer simply was not ruled by the success that adorned his life. He walked with God. His tombstone bears this simple epitaph: A Man of God. The secret—making the quiet place a priority.

THE QUIET TIME PLAN

Intimacy becomes radical when you become intentional with God—with a revolutionary plan to draw near to Him. Paul was very intentional: "I count all things to be loss in view of the surpassing value of knowing Christ Jesus my Lord, for whom I have suffered the loss of all things, and count them but rubbish so that I may gain Christ" (Philippians 3:8). Over the years, I have discovered certain disciplines of devotion in the Bible that help me become a participant, experiencing the character and person of the Lord in my own life. Henri Nouwen defines discipline as "the effort to create some space in which God can act."[4] Biblical devotional disciplines include such things as prayer, Bible study, meditating on God's Word, solitude, devotional reading, journaling, listening to God, submission to God, worship, and practical application. A quiet time plan embraces different devotional disciplines to draw you into God's Word so you can hear Him speak and respond to Him in prayer.

In Mark 9:29, Jesus makes a very important statement about prayer and quiet time in the context of the healing of a demon-possessed boy. Jesus admonishes His disciples, "This kind [of demon] cannot come out by anything but prayer." But when did Jesus pray? Luke 9:28 gives us the answer. It says that "[Jesus] took along Peter and John and James, and went up on the mountain to pray...while He was praying, the appearance of His face became different, and His clothing became white and gleaming." This event occurred just prior to the healing of the boy. When He speaks about prayer in this passage He is not referring to a single request offered to God, but an entire lifestyle, a habit of life.

He is talking about quiet time. *Prayer is first and foremost an ongoing, dynamic, intimate relationship with God that must be tended, nurtured, and cultivated through specific times of communion and fellowship with Him*...quiet time. That is why the word *PRAYER* is such a good way to remember how to spend time alone with the Lord.

The P.R.A.Y.E.R. Quiet Time Plan

Prepare Your Heart
Read and Study God's Word
Adore God in Prayer
Yield Yourself to God
Enjoy His Presence
Rest in His Love

- *Prepare Your Heart*—James 4:8 encourages you to "draw near to God and He will draw near to you." Prepare Your Heart includes simple prayer, solitude, silence, journaling, and spiritual meditation.

- *Read and Study God's Word*—In Colossians 3:16, Paul encourages you to "let the word of Christ richly dwell within you." Read and Study God's Word includes a Bible reading plan, observation, interpretation, and application.

- *Adore God in Prayer*—In 1 Thessalonians 5:17, Paul says to "pray without ceasing." Adore God in Prayer includes adoration, confession, thanksgiving, supplication, writing prayer requests, praying for the world, and praying Scripture.

- *Yield Yourself to God*—In 1 Peter 5:6, Peter says, "Humble yourselves under the mighty hand of God, that He may exalt you at the proper time." Yield Yourself to God includes humility, submission, brokenness, and surrender to God.

- *Enjoy His Presence*—The psalmist says, "Delight yourself in the LORD, and He will give you the desires of your heart" (Psalm 37:4). Enjoy His Presence includes practicing the presence of God as well as moment-by-moment prayer, extended times with the Lord, and personal retreats.

• *Rest in His Love*—Jesus said, "Come to Me, all who are weary and heavy-laden, and I will give you rest" (Matthew 11:28). Rest in His Love through sharing the life of Christ, discipleship, knowing the heart of Jesus, and bringing every part of your life to Him.

Once you learn the devotional disciplines of this quiet time plan, you will want to personalize it as the Lord leads you in your adventure with Him. This plan is flexible and may be used as a guideline whether you have ten minutes or two hours to spend with the Lord. It is a tool that is learned, practiced, and developed over a lifetime. With the time, the place, and the plan, quiet time is no longer a seemingly unattainable mystery but an exciting adventure. Quiet time is not an end in itself but a means to your desired goal: radical intimacy—the great adventure of knowing God.

My Response

DATE:

KEY VERSE: "But the news about Him was spreading even farther, and large crowds were gathering to hear Him and to be healed of their sicknesses. But Jesus Himself would often slip away to the wilderness and pray" (Luke 5:15-16).

FOR FURTHER THOUGHT: What is your favorite way to spend time alone with the Lord at the present time? What are you looking forward to learning as you read about this plan for quiet time?

Prepare Your Heart
Read and Study God's Word
Adore God in Prayer
Yield Yourself to God
Enjoy His Presence
Rest in His Love

MY RESPONSE:

Day Five

THE GRAND EXPERIMENT: QUIET TIME RESOURCES

So let us know, let us press on
to know the LORD.

HOSEA 6:3

⟶⟵

uiet time is the grand experiment. You can do something new in your quiet time every day and never exhaust the possibilities of devotion to God. Hosea said, "So let us know, let us press on to know the LORD. His going forth is as certain as the dawn; and He will come to us like the rain, like the spring rain watering the earth" (Hosea 6:3). Pressing on includes exploring the vast array of devotional materials available on the market today. Your quiet time resources will be the fuel for the fire of radical intimacy.

I remember browsing a Christian bookstore not long after I had made the decision to follow Christ, quite overwhelmed by the vast number of books. There were so many Bibles, I didn't even know where to start. I realized I could leave the bookstore with a whole bag of books and still not know where to begin my quiet time. How can a Christian make sense of all the available resources on the market today? The P.R.A.Y.E.R. Quiet Time Plan will become your shopping guide for resources at the Christian bookstore.

Buy the devotional *My Utmost for His Highest* to Prepare Your Heart. Find *Strong's Concordance* as a Bible study tool to Read and Study God's Word. Search out *31 Days of Praise* by Ruth Myers to Adore God in Prayer. Obtain *The Pursuit of God* by A.W. Tozer as a classic devotional reading to Yield Yourself to God. Browse the music section for Darlene Zschech's *Shout to the Lord* worship CD to Enjoy His Presence. Choose a small New Living Translation to help you memorize verses to Rest in His Love (see appendix 3: "P.R.A.Y.E.R. Quiet Time Plan Resource Guide").

YOUR BIBLE

The most important resource in your quiet time is a Bible that you can make your own. Your Bible will become a friend to you, for the words contained there will lead you to the heart of God as you learn about His character and His ways (Exodus 33:13). You can choose from general text Bibles (no cross-references), reference Bibles (includes cross-references), study Bibles (includes commentary notes), and devotional Bibles (includes a reading plan for the year). Many translations exist, including the King James Version, the New King James Version, the New International Version, the New American Standard Bible, the English Standard Version, the New Living Translation, the Good News Bible, The Message, the New Century Version, and the Amplified Bible.

How do you choose your everyday Bible to Read and Study God's Word?

- *Size*—Choose a size that is both transportable and readable. Some Bibles are so large that you need a piece of luggage to haul them around, and they're filled with study aids you may never use. Some Bibles are so small that you need a magnifying glass to read the type, making them improbable daily companions in your quiet time. I am a firm believer in taking your Bible everywhere you go, especially to church. The point is to interact with God in His Word. How can you underline significant verses unless you have your own personal Bible with you?

• *Translation*—Choose a translation that is understandable, memorable, and accurate. The five best translations on the market today are the New American Standard Bible, the English Standard Version, the New Living Translation, the New King James Version, and the New International Version. The New American Standard Bible, English Standard Version, and New King James Version are word-for-word translations (literal), and the New International Version and New Living Translation are thought-for-thought translations (dynamic equivalence). A word-for-word translation is excellent for word studies, and it helps you remember biblical verses. But it sometimes places words in odd locations in a verse, obscuring the meaning of the text. A thought-for-thought translation unfolds the meaning of the text and clarifies the original Greek or Hebrew. However, it may use different English words for the same Greek or Hebrew word, making it more difficult to do a word study or commit verses to memory. I personally use all five translations in my quiet time. In fact, I also use The Message, The Amplified Version, and others as well. To decide, browse a Christian bookstore and spend time comparing the same verses in many translations.

• *Type*—For your everyday Bible, choose a reference edition that has cross-references in the side or center margins. For in-depth study, choose a study Bible, containing study helps and commentary notes to explain the meanings of verses. My favorite study Bibles are the *NIV Study Bible,* the *Thompson Chain Reference Bible,* and the *New Inductive Study Bible* (NASB). For daily devotional reading, choose a devotional Bible offering a daily Bible reading plan. My favorite devotional Bibles are *The One Year Bible, The Daily*

Bible, and *The Oswald Chambers Daily Devotional Bible.* The great joy in choosing Bibles for your quiet time comes from allowing God to lead you in the choice and use of each one.

YOUR QUIET TIME NOTEBOOK

In your quiet time it is important to write down what you have learned—for memory, for meditation, and for comprehension. At minimum, use a spiral notebook from an office supply store. Eventually, progress to a comprehensive notebook with journal, Bible study, prayer request, personal application, cross-reference, and notes pages organized according to the P.R.A.Y.E.R. Quiet Time Plan. Quiet Time Ministries Press publishes *The Quiet Time Notebook,* which I developed over many years and which I personally use in my own quiet time. (See the Quiet Time Ministries Bookstore at www.quiettime.org.)

DEVOTIONAL READING

I have often been asked how to choose devotional reading for quiet time. The books you choose must contain references to God's Word, not just platitudes. A Scripture reference in your devotional reading may lead you to a vital passage for your life. My favorite devotional authors are A.W. Tozer, Andrew Murray, G. Campbell Morgan, F.B. Meyer, J.I. Packer, R.A. Torrey, E.M. Bounds, Amy Carmichael, Hannah Whitall Smith, Alan Redpath, and Oswald Chambers. My favorite devotional books include *My Utmost for His Highest* by Oswald Chambers, *The Edges of His Ways* by Amy Carmichael, *The Valley of Vision: A Collection of Puritan Prayers and Devotions*, and *Springs in the Valley* and *Streams in the Desert* by Mrs. Charles Cowman.

BIBLE STUDY TOOLS

As you grow in the Lord, add an exhaustive concordance in the same translation as your Bible and a word study tool, preferably the *Hebrew-Greek Word Study Bible* (NASB edition) by Spiros Zodhiates. My favorite concordance is the *NASB Exhaustive Concordance.*

MUSIC

My favorite worship CDs are by Stefanie Kelly, Mary Naman, Johnny Mann, Michael W. Smith, and Darlene Zschech. My favorite hymnbook is *Hymns for the Family of God.*

MISCELLANEOUS

- *Audiovisual*—Collect audio and videotapes and DVDs by your favorite Bible teachers. Some of my favorites include Josh McDowell, Bill Bright, Charles Stanley, R.C. Sproul, Zola Levitt, Jill Briscoe, Anne Graham Lotz, and Tim LaHaye.

- *Bible studies*—Quiet Time Ministries, NavPress, Bible Study Fellowship, Community Bible Study, Precept Ministries International, and Campus Crusade for Christ all publish Bible studies for small groups.

- *Reading glasses*

- *Tissues*

- *Glue stick*

- *Index cards*—Use 3 x 5 index cards to memorize Scripture, to record principles you learn in your quiet time for review throughout the day, and to write key verses for your prayer time.

- *Bookmarks*

- *Pens and pencils*—My favorite colored pens for Bible marking are the Pigma Micron 6-pack color set, which can be obtained at any art or crafts store.

YOUR QUIET TIME AREA

Gather all your quiet time materials together in your quiet place. I like to keep all of my materials in a quiet time basket—just a simple basket with a handle, strong and sturdy enough to hold my books. In that basket I have my Bible, *The Quiet Time Notebook,* devotional reading, a hymnbook, word study tools, a small commentary, a CD player, worship CDs, tissues, and reading glasses. I can take my basket to any room in the house or outside on the patio. When I leave home to speak at a retreat, I take my quiet time basket with me. Everything I need is in one place. A basket, a shelf, a bedside table…it's your choice. Make it your own.

My Response

DATE:

KEY VERSE: "So let us know, let us press on to know the LORD" (Hosea 6:3).

FOR FURTHER THOUGHT: What materials do you use in your quiet time right now? What do you want to add to that collection of resources for your quiet time? What is your favorite Bible to use in your quiet time? What is your favorite tool in your quiet time right now?

MY RESPONSE:

Day Six

QUIET TIME—
WEEK ONE:
THE GREAT ADVENTURE

If you are pleased with me, teach me
your ways so I may know you and
continue to find favor with you.

EXODUS 33:13 NIV

PREPARE YOUR HEART

To embark on the pursuit of knowing God is to launch out on a great adventure. This great adventure produces a great heart for God. History has seen many great hearts. One such person was Amy Carmichael, who, at the age of 17, purposed in her heart to follow Jesus wherever He led and to surrender all to know Him. This decision enabled her to take part in the great adventure that only great hearts can know. At the age of 33, Amy left the comforts of home and traveled to Dohnavur,

India, as a missionary. One day, while drinking tea in Pannaivilai, a village in southern India, she was visited by a friend and a 7-year-old girl. This young girl had escaped from the Hindu temple where she was to become one of the "Davadasis" or temple prostitutes. Amy lifted the girl up on her lap and spoke softly to her, saying, "What a brave little soul you have, Preena." Amy hugged and kissed her. This affection was new to Preena, whose own mother had sent her to the temple. "Amma, I want to stay with you always," sobbed Preena. That was when Amy realized her life work: rescuing hundreds of these children from temple prostitution in India. Amy became "Amma" to so many there in India, and numerous people came to know Christ personally. None of this would have happened had Amy not made the decision to know the Lord so many years before. That decision altered the course of her life and resulted in changed lives throughout the world. Will you be one of those "great hearts" like Amy Carmichael? Begin your quiet time with simple prayer, asking the Lord to quiet your heart that you might hear Him speak in His Word.

READ AND STUDY GOD'S WORD

1. The Bible is filled with men and women who experienced the great adventure of knowing God. Moses is one of those who knew a radical intimacy with God. We learn from Exodus 33:11 (NIV) that "the Lord would speak to Moses face to face, as a man speaks with his friend." That phrase "face to face" means person to person, heart to heart. It implies an intimate fellowship and exchange of thought and emotion. Read Exodus 33:7–34:9 and record everything you see about the intimate relationship between God and Moses. What do you notice in their conversations and actions? Write your insights in the space provided.

2. Describe the relationship between God and Moses.

3. What did Moses learn about God as he spent time with Him?

4. What is your favorite verse in this passage of Scripture? Underline it in your Bible and write it out in the space provided. You may even want to begin to memorize it.

5. Summarize what you have learned from your time in God's Word and from the example of Amy Carmichael that helps you in your great adventure of knowing God.

Adore God in Prayer

Will you pray the prayer of Moses today? "If you are pleased with me, teach me your ways so I may know you and continue to find favor with you" (Exodus 33:13 NIV).

Yield Yourself to God

"The *Lord* shall guide thee." Not an angel, but JEHOVAH shall guide thee. He said he would not go through the wilderness before his people, an angel should go before them to lead them in the way; but Moses said, "If *thy* presence go not with me, carry us not up hence." Christian, God has not left you in your earthly pilgrimage to an angel's guidance: he himself leads the van. You may not see the cloudy, fiery pillar, but Jehovah will never forsake you. Notice the word *shall*—"The Lord shall guide thee." How certain this makes it! How sure it is that God will not forsake us! His precious "shalls" and "wills" are better than men's oaths. "I will never leave thee, nor forsake thee." Then observe the adverb *continually*. We are not merely to be guided sometimes, but we are to have a perpetual monitor; not occasionally to be left to our own understanding, and so to wander, but we are continually to hear the guiding voice of the Great Shepherd; and if we follow close at his heels, we shall not err, but be led by a right way to a city to dwell in. If you have to change your position in life; if you have to emigrate to distant shores; if it should happen that you are cast into poverty, or uplifted suddenly into a more responsible position than the one you now occupy; if you are thrown among strangers, or cast among foes, yet tremble not, for "the Lord shall guide thee continually." There are no dilemmas out of which you shall not be delivered if you live near to God, and your heart be kept warm with holy love. He goes not amiss who goes in the company of God. Like Enoch, walk with God, and you cannot mistake your road. You have infallible wisdom to direct you, immutable love to comfort you, and eternal power to defend you. "Jehovah"—mark the word—"Jehovah shall guide thee continually."[1]

Charles Haddon Spurgeon
Morning and Evening

Enjoy His Presence

What adventure is awaiting you, and what life work will be the result of your pursuit of God? As you seek the favor of the Lord as Moses did, your life will shine with radiance, and those around you will be drawn to Christ. Will you close your time with the Lord by expressing all that is on your heart as you think about your own intimacy with Him?

Rest in His Love

"And the Lord replied to Moses, 'I will indeed do what you have asked, for you have found favor with me, and you are my friend'" (Exodus 33:17 NLT).

Notes—Week One

Week Two

BEGIN
THE CLIMB

Days 7-12

Day Seven

SECRET ONE:
PREPARE YOUR HEART

*Draw near to God
and He will draw near to you.*

JAMES 4:8

⟋⟍

reparation is the foundation of radical intimacy. In fact, your experience with God may be measured in terms of your initial preparation. James says, "Draw near to God and He will draw near to you" (James 4:8).

When I was in college I had one philosophy for my studies: Wait until the last minute. One Person changed my whole attitude toward preparation: the Lord Jesus Christ. By the time I began seminary in 1987, I was prepared to study hard, read volumes of material, and write lengthy papers on theological issues. For example, in my Revelation class I presented a thorough dissertation on the second coming of Christ. I looked up all the important Greek words, studied Revelation

19, completed observation and cross-reference studies, and read commentaries. I timed and practiced my presentation to the exact second, weaving in overhead transparencies and illustrations. When the moment came to walk up to the lectern, instead of my heart pounding with fear, I reached the podium in quiet assurance. I was prepared.

The initial element of the P.R.A.Y.E.R. Quiet Time Plan is "Prepare Your Heart." This sets the tone for all that follows. The goal is to quiet your heart, slow down to hear God speak, and ask God to open your spiritual eyes and ears and to give you a teachable spirit. Jeremiah says, "Blessed is the man who trusts in the LORD and whose trust is the LORD. For he will be like a tree planted by the water, that extends its roots by a stream and will not fear when the heat comes; but its leaves will be green, and it will not be anxious in a year of drought nor cease to yield fruit" (Jeremiah 17:7-8). God will enable you to outlast the droughts of life by planting you in an ideal place by the water where you may flourish. The stream of water is the Lord Himself, "the fountain of living water" (Jeremiah 17:13). Your responsibility as one who "trusts in the Lord" is to extend your roots by the stream. When you prepare your heart, you actively reach out and draw near to God like that tree planted by the stream.

What kind of preparation matters most to God? David, the man after God's own heart, was filled with a great desire to build a house for God—a place where he and others could go to meet with God. This desire pleased God immensely, but God said no to David and instead assigned the task to David's son Solomon. David instructed Solomon and the leaders of Israel in the building of the temple. He focused on preparation—not only material preparation but also spiritual preparation.

David told the leaders to "set your heart and your soul to seek the LORD your God" (1 Chronicles 22:19). From this verse we see that the place of the pursuit of God is in the heart and soul. Spiritual life with God is an *inner life.* The Hebrew conception of man applies here. The Israelites believed that man is composed of the inner self and the outer appearance, that is, what one is to oneself and how one appears to those who observe him. The soul is the inner person. The heart is the totality of your inner nature: your emotions, thoughts, and will. It is who you really are—no trappings, no masks—the *you* that God sees. Meeting with God daily is a daring and vulnerable venture because you are exposing to your heavenly Father the real "you" that can be touched and moved and changed.

The heart and soul is the place where you commune with God and truly experience Him, the place where you may touch the hem of His garments. And what a broad place it is, capable of holding deep emotion and grasping awe-inspiring spiritual truth. No wonder Jesus said rivers of living water can flow from your innermost being—a real experience of renewal (John 7:37-38). The Holy Spirit indwells your heart and soul and fills you with the love of God. In essence, the heart and soul provide the place where God now dwells with you. This is the great mystery: "Christ in you, the hope of glory" (Colossians 1:27).

What does it mean to "set your heart" (1 Chronicles 22:19)? The Hebrew word means to focus your attention on the activity of seeking the Lord. Focus your mind, your thoughts, your emotions, and your will. Why would David give the leaders of Israel this directive? They were about to embark on the greatest task of their lives: building God's temple. David wanted them to know that the primary imperative in life was to focus on God and draw near to Him. If you will prepare your heart, you will have a heart that *dares to draw near,* as James implies when he says, "Draw near to God and He will draw near to you" (James 4:8).

Drawing near to God requires a daring heart because after you draw near to the living God you will never be the same. John White writes in *Daring to Draw Near,* "We confuse intimacy with its counterfeit, familiarity...intimacy is what we want but familiarity is all we achieve... Intimacy is dangerous, a knowing and being known deeply and profoundly...it involves being humble enough to share the secrets of your heart."[1] This is the value of preparing our hearts. It gives us the space to let down our guard in the presence of our Father that we might commune with Him and hear Him speak.

Why do we need to focus on God? Because we live in a distracting world. When you focus on God, you will find that your view of God is enlarged, the things of the earth will grow strangely dim, and a passion for God within your heart is revived. You are focused and ready to hear what God has to say.

I was talking to a businessman about this idea of preparing your heart. He said that in the morning he rarely feels like spending time with God. By taking a few moments at the beginning of his quiet time to prepare his heart, he finds his thoughts, emotions, and will focused on the things of the Lord. This preparation gives him the energy and the will to pursue God through study of the Word and prayer.

What will focus your thoughts, emotions, and will on God so that you are ready to listen to Him? Preparing your heart includes the disciplines of simple prayer, solitude and silence, journaling, and Christian meditation.

Amy Carmichael was a missionary in India for more than 50 years who experienced deep suffering. If you listen to the words of this prayer by Amy Carmichael, you will hear the beat of a heart that dared to draw near to God.

> From prayer that asks that I may be
> Sheltered from winds that beat on Thee,
> From fearing when I should aspire,
> From faltering when I should climb higher,
> From silken self, O Captain, free
> Thy soldier who would follow Thee.
>
> From subtle love of softening things,
> From easy choices, weakenings
> (Not thus are spirits fortified,
> Not this way went the Crucified),
> From all that dims Thy Calvary,
> O Lamb of God deliver me.
>
> Give me the love that leads the way,
> The faith that nothing can dismay,
> The hope no disappointments tire,
> The passion that will burn like fire;
> Let me not sink to be a clod:
> Make me Thy fuel, O Flame of God.[2]

My Response

DATE:

KEY VERSE: "Draw near to God and He will draw near to you" (James 4:8).

FOR FURTHER THOUGHT: As you think about all that you read today, what is the great value of preparation in your quiet time? Why do you need to prepare your heart? What is your favorite way to prepare your heart?

MY RESPONSE:

Day Eight

SIMPLE PRAYER, SOLITUDE, AND SILENCE

He turned to me and heard my cry.

PSALM 40:1 NIV

⌇∞

Prayer quickly takes you to the heart of God. David knew this when he said, "He turned to me and heard my cry" (Psalm 40:1 NIV). When you pray a simple prayer, anticipation and excitement grow inside of you. Your heart quickly moves from apathy to interest, from the temporal to the eternal. Your simple prayer will soften your heart and draw your attention to Him, preparing you to sit down with Him and hear Him speak in His Word. You can count on the promise in 2 Corinthians 3:16: "Whenever a person turns to the Lord, the veil is taken away." The eyes of your heart are open to the Lord, and you will see His character and ways.

Simple prayers are one or two-sentence prayers to the Lord. The book of Psalms is filled with simple prayers.

- "Search me, O God, and know my heart; try me and know my anxious thoughts; and see if there be any hurtful way in me, and lead me in the everlasting way" (Psalm 139:23-24).

- "Give ear to my words, O LORD, consider my groaning. Heed the sound of my cry for help, my King and my God, for to You I pray" (Psalm 5:1-2).

- "I love You, O LORD, my strength" (Psalm 18:1).

- "Make me know Your ways, O LORD; teach me Your paths. Lead me in Your truth and teach me, for You are the God of my salvation; for You I wait all the day" (Psalm 25:4-5).

I like to talk with the Lord about everything I read in my quiet time. I ask Him questions, such as "What does that mean, Lord?" or "Lord, are You trying to tell me something here?" I might respond to something I've read in my devotional reading and say "Lord, that is amazing! Thank You for showing that to me!" Then I might say, "But Lord, how do I express that in my life?" Sometimes your simple prayer will be high and lofty as you dare to dream big dreams with your Lord. And sometimes your simple prayer will be exactly that—very simple. You might just say "Thank You, Lord." When you wake in the morning, be aware of your Lord's presence. In fact, you might say "Good morning, Lord. This is the day You have made; I will rejoice and be glad in it."

You can practice simple prayer all day long, from the time you wake to the time you rest your head on your pillow at night. Cultivate the habit of simple prayer, an ongoing dialogue with your Lord throughout your quiet time. Quiet time is not something that you do outside the presence of the Lord. It is not that God is way out there in the universe and you are tucked away in a crevice here on earth. He is right here with you now. Talk with Him. Express your heart to Him. That is simple prayer.

SOLITUDE AND SILENCE

Solitude and silence shut out the world and open the heart to God. No wonder God said, "Be still, and know that I am God" (Psalm 46:10 NIV). Solitude and silence give you the ability to hear God's voice.

When I graduated from seminary, my husband took me on a trip to Yosemite National Park. I love the majesty of the mountains, the sound of the wind blowing through the pine trees, and the birds chirping their melodies. It made me feel as though I had a little taste of heaven. One day, the Lord did something special for me. It snowed. Now that may not seem too exciting to you, but for a girl from Phoenix who often endured 120-degree heat, snow is an amazing experience. Everyone at the hotel was complaining about the snow in June. But I grabbed my Bible, put on warm clothes and good hiking boots, and launched out to enjoy this wonderful beauty with the Lord. As I walked along the path into the forest, it began snowing more heavily, and I took cover under the branches of a tall pine. How deafening was the silence as the snow blanketed the ground and weighed down the branches of the trees. Then, a new sound came from that silence—a spiritual peace that seemed to flood my soul. The solitude I experienced in that moment produced a serenity that drew my thoughts to the Lord. In that time, I learned the value of solitude and silence for the heart and soul.

What are solitude and silence? Don Whitney defines them in his book *Spiritual Disciplines for the Christian Life*. "It is the Spiritual Discipline of voluntarily and temporarily withdrawing to privacy for spiritual purposes…The period of solitude may last only a few minutes or for days. As with silence, solitude may be sought in order to participate without interruption in other Spiritual Disciplines, or just to be alone with God."[1]

Solitude and silence slow you down, blocking out the distractions of life. The heart needs quiet time to focus more fully on God. Even Jesus sought solitude. Mark tells us, "In the early morning, while it was still dark, Jesus got up…and went away to a secluded place, and was praying there" (Mark 1:35). In Luke 5:16 we see that Jesus would often withdraw to lonely places to pray. A.W. Tozer says, "May not the inadequacy of much of our spiritual experience be traced back to our habit of skipping through the corridors of the Kingdom like children through the marketplace, chattering about everything, but pausing to learn the true value of nothing?"[2] Silence and solitude will encourage you to pause for quiet time, where you will learn lifechanging, spiritual truth from God.

As others have said before, we have become a generation of people who worship our work, who work at our play, and who play at our worship. To find solitude and silence with determination means that you are serious about knowing God. Listen to what God says: "In repentance and rest you will be saved, in quietness and trust is your strength" (Isaiah 30:15).

The profound nature of solitude and silence is demonstrated when Elijah was on the mountain of Horeb alone with God. When did Elijah hear the voice of the Lord? Not in the great and powerful winds, the earthquake tearing the mountains apart, or even the flaming fire. No, the Lord was not in any of those things. It was only as Elijah stood at the entrance of a cave—in the solitude and silence of a gentle wind—that he finally heard the voice of the Lord (1 Kings 19:11-13).

How are you going to find solitude and silence in your life? Ask the Lord. Finding a quiet place of solitude is the first step and will help you learn to be still before the Lord. Although you may have a life right now where privacy may seem impossible, again, ask the Lord. He will show you the way. One of my friends with small children gets up very early and tiptoes past the children's rooms to the kitchen, where her Bible is already open, waiting for her. Another friend can find privacy in only one room of her house—the bathroom. Be inventive. Be determined. If one idea does not work, try another. Remember, you are engaging in the grand experiment of quiet time.

Sometimes I retreat to the back porch even in 100-degree heat because it is the place where I can find the most solitude. At other times, I may easily find my quiet place in my study, my office, at a park, or at a mountain retreat. Your heart needs moments of silence, moments of solitude. When you begin your quiet time, you may choose to sit in silence for a few moments, allowing your thoughts to turn to the Lord and away from the world. The stillness will bring healing and comfort to your soul. In this silence, you may hear God speak.

May you experience the words of Robert Murray McCheyne:

> May you have a time of refreshing from the presence of the Lord! May He be the third with you who joined the two disciples on the way to Emmaus, and made their hearts burn by opening to them the Scriptures concerning

Himself...May your mind be solemnized, my dear friend, by the thought that we are ministers but for a time; that the Master may summon us to retire into silence, or may call us to the temple above; or the midnight cry of the great Bridegroom may break suddenly on our ears. Blessed is the servant that is found waiting! Make all your services tell for eternity; speak what you can look back upon with comfort when you must be silent.[3]

My Response

DATE:

KEY VERSE: "In the morning, O Lord, You will hear my voice; in the morning I will order my prayer to You and eagerly watch" (Psalm 5:3).

FOR FURTHER THOUGHT: Will you choose one of the simple prayers from this day's reading and write it out in the space provided here? What simple prayer expresses the desire of your heart today? What is your favorite place to find silence and solitude?

MY RESPONSE:

Day Nine

YOUR JOURNAL

My heart overflows with a good theme;
I address my verses to the King;
my tongue is the pen of a ready writer.

PSALM 45:1

⁓

ournaling pours your soul out to the Lord. When you journal, you become receptive to the voice of God. The psalmist said, "My heart overflows with a good theme; I address my verses to the King; my tongue is the pen of a ready writer" (Psalm 45:1). Writing in your journal prepares your heart to meet with God and express your deepest spiritual insights.

Certain Christian authors excite my soul: A.W. Tozer, Oswald Chambers, Amy Carmichael. Henri Nouwen was a priest and pastor of the twentieth century, a prolific author, and a professor at several theological institutes and universities. In his last years, he ministered to handicapped adults in Toronto, Canada. What I appreciate about his writing is his deep expression of love for Christ and his deeper spiritual life. His writings have a unique style that communicates a great sense of peace and joy. Prior to his death in 1996, he released for publication what he called his "secret journal." He said he wrote it during the most difficult time of his life, a time of extreme anguish when he wondered whether he would be able to hold on to life itself.

He says in his journal, "Everything came crashing down—my self esteem, my energy to live and work, my sense of being loved, my hope for healing, my trust in God...everything. Here I was, a writer about the spiritual life, known as someone who loves God and gives hope to people, flat on the ground and in total darkness."[1] He later writes, "To my surprise, I never lost the ability to write. In fact, writing became part of my struggle for survival. It gave me the little distance from myself that I needed to keep from drowning in my despair."[2]

Each day he wrote spiritual imperatives and encouragements to himself in his journal. He says that eight years later he was able to look back on that time as intense purification that led him gradually to a new inner freedom, a new hope, and a new creativity.

In her book *Journaling*, Ann Broyles shares a story called "Maggie's Journal." In that story, a grandmother gives a journal to a young girl who is facing a summer with a broken leg. The grandmother says this to Maggie:

> It's a journal, Maggie, a special place for you to put down all the special things you think or see or dream, anytime you want. When you are in a rotten mood and your brain is full of cobwebs, or when life is so marvelous you feel like you're soaring in a balloon, you can put it all down in your journal. You can go through your own looking glass, Maggie, and find your wonderland...Writing in your journal helps you see things you never thought about before...Soon, each day seems full of small marvels you must write down."[3]

I cannot remember where I first discovered journaling. It just seemed to be natural for me. I've always written my thoughts on pieces of paper, in notebooks...anywhere I could find a space for words and ideas that came from my heart. I do, however, remember when I became serious about journaling. In my last year in college I read a powerful book called

The Shadow of the Almighty, compiled by Elisabeth Elliot, containing excerpts from her husband's journal. Her husband, Jim Elliot, was one of five missionaries who were all martyred in Ecuador by Auca Indians. In Jim Elliot's journal, I discovered what it means to have a heart for God and an intense passion for Christ. There I found these powerful words: "He is no fool who gives up what he cannot keep to gain what he cannot lose." He wrote this prayer to the Lord: "God, I pray, light up these idle sticks of my life and may I burn up for Thee. Consume my life, My God, for it is Thine. I seek not a long life but a full one like yours, Lord Jesus." Journaling was something that Jim Elliot did to help him wrestle with spiritual truth, pray to God, and express his love for God. As a result, he grew spiritually in his relationship with his Lord.

After I read *The Shadow of the Almighty* I became very intentional about writing in my journal. I purposed in my heart to get a journal that I would begin to use in my quiet time as a method of expression to God and a way to dialogue about spiritual truth.

Outside of prayer and the Word of God, writing in a journal has helped me most to grow spiritually in my relationship with the Lord. Your journal can become a tool to prepare your heart and slow you down so you can begin to hear God speak in His Word.

The life of Hannah, described in 1 Samuel, can help us understand the value of journaling. Hannah experienced what St. John of the Cross called "the dark night of the soul." She wanted more than anything to have a child. She prayed, asking God for the gift of a child. Nothing happened. In the temple, she threw herself at the mercy of God and begged Him to hear her prayer. She was so fervent, emotional, and wholehearted in her request that the priest thought she had been drinking. In 1 Samuel 1:15-16, Hannah told Eli, the priest, that she was deeply troubled and that she had not been drinking. She said, "I was pouring out my soul to the Lord." After her outpouring of emotion, Hannah was a different woman: "She went her way and ate something, and her face was no longer downcast."

Your relationship with the Lord is the most intimate relationship you can have in life. Why? Because it involves the heart and soul. Your soul can quite easily become downcast, burdened, anguished, and grieving; God desires response, requests, and dialogue from us. When you pour out your soul to Him, the result is intimacy. That intimacy with God brings peace and a sense of well-being because He hears, He cares, and He comforts.

What is the spiritual basis for pouring out your soul to the Lord?

- Your life with the Lord is an inner life.

- Your life with the Lord requires openness, transparency, and vulnerability.

- Your life with the Lord requires interaction and dialogue with Him.

What does it mean to pour out your soul to the Lord? The Hebrew word *shaphak* means to "bare one's soul." It comes from the idea of pouring out the contents of a vessel.

- It is an expression of trust in God (Psalm 62:8).

- It is what you do to find refuge in God (Psalm 62:8).

- It is what you are to do in times of need and in times when no one seems to care (Psalm 42:2-3).

- It involves remembering God as He has worked powerfully in the past (Psalm 42:4-5).

- It is how you find rest in God (Psalm 62:8).

- It involves meditating on the works of God (Psalm 143:5).

- It is accomplished in the presence of the Lord (Lamentations 2:19).

Pouring out your soul to the Lord means to lift up every desire, need, joy, sorrow, and thought that is on your heart and in your mind to your Father who loves you more than you can imagine. It is done in the presence of God, directed to God, and intended for the glory of God. A.W. Tozer speaks of the importance of developing this inner life with the Lord: "We should press on to enjoy in personal inward experience the exalted privileges that are ours in Christ Jesus: that we should insist upon tasting the sweetness of internal worship in spirit as well as in truth..."[4]

How can you learn to pour out your soul? One of the best ways is by learning to journal. The Bible itself provides the greatest example of a journal—the book of Psalms. The book of Psalms is a journal of the saints to God. David, in one of his journal entries, says in Psalm 42:4, "These things I remember and I pour out my soul within me." In 62:8 (NIV), David writes, "Trust in him at all times, O people; pour out your hearts to him, for God is our refuge."

THE EXPERIENCE OF JOURNALING

Journaling is not an *exercise* but an *experience*—an experience with God. You journal in the presence of God, to God, and for the glory of God, all within the framework of human language. Journaling is a spiritual journey of reflection and discovery, opening up the world of quiet time to deeper insight into God's Word. Your journal should contain dialogue with God, insights about God, questions for God, complaints, goals, and ideas. As Ann Broyles shares in her book *Journaling*, "Each of us carries on inner conversations as we sort through our feelings about daily living, our relationships, world events. Journaling is the process of writing down those 'talks with ourselves' so that what our mind is thinking and our heart is feeling becomes tangible: ink on paper."[5] Journaling should become like talking with a good friend. Writing in your journal is a way of drawing near to remember God and find your refuge in Him. The result is peace, spiritual growth, and intimacy with God.

Some may say, "I'm not the journaling type. I'm not a writer. I hate to write." When I hear those words, I remember the great men and women of God who have kept journals in one form or another. These include the apostle Paul, Martin Luther, A.W. Tozer, Amy Carmichael, Jim Elliot, Charles Haddon Spurgeon, George Whitefield, John Wesley, and Elisabeth Elliot. I love to write in my journal, but I do not do it every day. You do not need to feel as though you have to fill a page up in your journal. If you are just beginning the adventure of journaling, you might consider just writing a one-sentence prayer to begin your quiet time. Or write out one verse or insight that was significant to you in your quiet time.

LEARNING TO JOURNAL

How can you learn to journal? First, read the journals of Jim Elliot, Amy Carmichael, George Whitefield, and John Wesley. My favorites are *The Shadow of the Almighty* and *The Journals of Jim Elliot* by Elisabeth Elliot and *The Edges of His Ways* by Amy Carmichael. Examine what they wrote. Try to imagine why they wrote it. Search for insights on how to apply their methods and their styles through your own personality.

Second, experiment. You may select a simple spiral-bound notebook with lined note paper and a ballpoint pen, or you may prefer a fancy leather book of fine stationery with quill and ink. Better yet, open your laptop, bring up a Word document, and type away. I am partial to the style of *The Quiet Time Notebook* published by Quiet Time Ministries Press. You might think of *The Quiet Time Notebook* as a comprehensive journal with six unique sections. You can write your thoughts in the first section, respond to the Word of God in the second section, write out prayers in the third section, apply what you've learned in the fourth section, write insights from Bible study in the fifth section, and journal your responses and interaction with devotional reading, tapes, and sermons in the sixth section (see Figure 1).

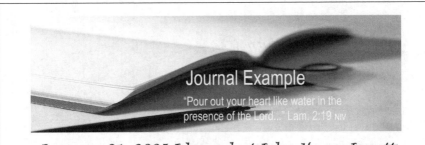

Journal Example

"Pour out your heart like water in the presence of the Lord..." Lam. 2:19 NIV

January 21, 2005 I love what John Henry Jowett says today in "The Things Which Lead To Peace." He says there is a great reward for meditation and obedience. "The God of peace shall be with you." He goes on to say, "And that is everything. If the King is present at the table, a crust is a feast. If the Lord is on the battlefield, then amid all the surrounding turbulence there is a centre of peace. When the God of peace is in the life there is a chamber in which the sound of warfare never comes." I have truly experienced that what Jowett says is true. My relationship with the Lord is that one thing no one and nothing can touch.

Figure 1. Journal page from *The Quiet Time Notebook*.

My Response

DATE:

KEY VERSE: "My tongue is the pen of a ready writer" (Psalm 45:1).

FOR FURTHER THOUGHT: How can your journal provide a great way to prepare your heart? What are you going to use for a journal in your quiet time?

MY RESPONSE:

Day Ten

WRITING IN
YOUR JOURNAL

When he [the king] takes the throne of
his kingdom, he is to write for himself
on a scroll a copy of this law.

DEUTERONOMY 17:18 NIV

⟿

What will you write in your journal? Start with the Word of God. Write a verse or even a complete chapter from the Bible that has been significant to you. There is supernatural power in writing the Word of God in your journal (Hebrews 4:12). When you physically write the Word of God, you impress it on your heart and on your mind. As you write, you will focus your thoughts on what God is saying in His Word.

In Deuteronomy 17:18-20 (NIV), God commanded the future kings of Israel to write out a copy of the Scripture, to keep it with them, and to read it all the days of their lives.

When he [the king] takes the throne of his kingdom, he is to write for himself on a scroll a copy of this law, taken from that of the priests, who are Levites. It is to be with him, and he is to read it all the days of his life so that he may learn to revere the LORD his God and follow carefully all the words of this law and these decrees and not consider himself better than his brothers and turn from the law to the right or to the left. Then he and his descendants will reign a long time over his kingdom in Israel.

God made promises to the future kings of Israel who would write out Scripture in a journal:

- The king would learn to revere the Lord.

- The king would be obedient to God.

- The king would stay humble.

- The king would not turn from God's Word.

- The king and his descendents would reign a long time.

Writing out the Word of God transforms you from a spectator to a participant in the biblical message given by God.

As I begin my quiet time, I often write out a favorite verse from a psalm that has been significant to me. Often, I will write out complete psalms, personalizing them as if I had written the words myself. You might replace the personal pronouns "I" and "me" with your own name.

Here is an example from Psalm 23: "Lord, You are *my* shepherd; *I* will never want. You make *me* lie down in green pastures." From Psalm 31: "Be merciful to *me*, Lord, for *I* am in distress; *my* eyes grow weak with sorrow, *my* soul and *my* body with grief…*I* trust in You, O Lord, *I* say, 'You are *my* God.' *My* times are in Your hands; deliver *me* from *my* enemies and from those who pursue *me*. Let Your face shine on *me*, Your servant. Save *me* in Your unfailing love." And then I might pray, "O Lord, Your love for *me* is unfailing; You will never fail *me* or forsake *me*."

As I encounter a verse in my quiet time that ministers to me or challenges me, I make a special effort to write it in my journal. I always include the date so I can retrace my spiritual journey. As I write out the Word of God, I reflect on its meaning. What is God saying to me? Write out your insights and observations on the written Scripture. I either record these observations in the "Journal" section of *The Quiet Time Notebook* or reserve them for the "Read and Study" section. In this way, you can go back and see exactly what you learned about any given passage of Scripture. You are creating your own Bible commentary reference work.

Write Your Response to Scripture

How will you respond to God's Word? View the Scripture as a question that must be answered. Create questions from your study verse and then write your answers. This is where you can really dialogue with God in your journal. You may respond by writing a simple prayer, by making a deeper commitment to God about something that needs to be changed in your life, or simply by expressing your love and adoration for God's sovereignty. Of course, you may write a paragraph thanking God for what you are learning in your quiet time.

Write Your Burdens and God's Perspective

Write out the burdens of your heart in your journal. I like to answer the question that God asked Adam and Eve: "Where are you?" (Genesis 3:9). In essence, God asked Adam and Eve, "Where are you *with Me?*" God wanted Adam and Eve to communicate their thoughts with Him. Often, I will unburden my heart and pour out my soul to the Lord about what is going on in my life. I usually do this to prepare my heart at the beginning of my quiet time. After writing about your own circumstances, always remember to move on to God's perspective of your situation, which you can find in God's Word. Otherwise, frustrating circumstances will continually hinder you. Talk with the Lord about what is burdening your heart, but don't stop there. Hannah's life illustrated this idea as she looked to God's perspective, knowing that He had her life in His hands. After emptying her heart, she was able to hear the words of Eli: "Go in peace; and may the God of Israel grant your petition that you have asked of Him." These are my favorite verses addressing God's perspective:

- "I know the plans I have for you" (Jeremiah 29:11).

- "My God will supply all your needs" (Philippians 4:19).

- "And the God of all grace, who called you to his eternal glory in Christ, after you have suffered a little while, will himself restore you and make you strong, firm and steadfast" (1 Peter 5:10 NIV).

- "Can a woman forget her nursing child, and have no compassion on the son of her womb? Even these may forget, but I will not forget you. Behold, I have inscribed you on the palms of My hands; your walls are continually before Me" (Isaiah 49:15-16).

WRITE YOUR RESPONSE TO DEVOTIONAL READING

A good way to prepare your heart is to read the devotional works of other men and women who have known and loved God. Dialogue with their thoughts by interacting with them on paper. Write the most significant quotes in your journal and then write out how their thoughts impact your own life just as if you were sitting with them face-to-face, discussing their texts. You might also journal and dialogue with authors in the margin of their books. This discipline will make your devotional books treasures to cherish over the years.

WRITE YOUR PRAYERS

My favorite way to write in my journal is to write out my own prayers. I often do this both at the beginning and end of my quiet time. During times when you struggle with praying, especially in troubling life situations, writing out your prayers to the Lord might be easier. Let the words flow from your heart to the journal page. Don't stop to edit the prayer in your mind. Allow God the freedom of using your pen as a means of instruction. Then read and reflect on the prayer you have written.

WRITE YOUR HEART

Ultimately, write what is on your heart. The sky's the limit. You may include descriptions of life events and experiences or your feelings about a present situation and God's perspective. Journal your insights into the beauty of God's creation. Write a list of daily blessings. Write about what God is teaching you in your quiet time. Write about ministry ideas, lecture outlines, or magazine articles. Include prayers, psalms, poetry, stories, quotes, art, pencil sketches, and photography. Pour out your dreams, desires, and goals.

THE BENEFITS OF JOURNALING

What are the benefits of writing in your journal?

- It slows you down to listen to God and hear Him speak.
- It will give you a new appreciation of God's activity in your daily life.
- It clarifies your beliefs and leads to growth.
- It clarifies your goals and gives you a clearer sense of priorities.
- It can provide a release of emotions.
- It helps you gain godly perspective in life situations.
- It provides an avenue of self-expression and creativity.
- It provides a chronicle of your spiritual journey with God.
- It helps you work through problems.
- It encourages intimacy with God.

Hannah poured out her soul to the Lord. Before she did, she was in great anguish and grief with a downcast soul. Afterward, she was able to go her way and eat something, and her face was no longer downcast. Hannah received God's grace. Not only did she receive her request for a son, Samuel, but after she dedicated Samuel to the Lord, Hannah received God's blessing of five more children. Her sorrow was turned to joy. Her prayer is recorded for all of us in 1 Samuel 2:1-2 (NIV): "My heart rejoices in the LORD, in the LORD my horn is lifted high. My mouth boasts over my enemies, for I delight in your deliverance. There is no one holy like the LORD; there is no one besides you; there is no Rock like our God."

Will you pour out your soul to the Lord? Openness and vulnerability with the Lord are parts of radical intimacy. Learn to write in your journal. It will become a spiritual legacy and a testimony to God's work in your life. Your journal can be a tool that will so prepare your heart that you will be ready to hear God's Word and be a living testimony to His work in your life. Oh, may our hearts echo this prayer that Jim Elliot wrote in his journal: "Lord, make our way prosperous, not that we achieve high station, but that our lives may be an exhibit to the great value of knowing God. In Jesus' name, Amen."

DATE:

KEY VERSE: "When he [the king] takes the throne of his kingdom, he is to write for himself on a scroll a copy of this law, taken from that of the priests, who are Levites. It is to be with him, and he is to read it all the days of his life so that he may learn to revere the LORD His God and follow carefully all the words of this law and these decrees and not consider himself better than his brothers and turn from the law to the right or to the left. Then he and his descendants will reign a long time over his kingdom in Israel" (Deuteronomy 17:18-20 NIV).

FOR FURTHER THOUGHT: What kinds of things can you write in your journal? What is your favorite way to journal? Will you write a prayer today expressing all that is on your heart?

MY RESPONSE:

Day Eleven

CHRISTIAN
MEDITATION

I remember the days of old.
I ponder all your great works.
I think about what you have done.

PSALM 143:5 NLT

*T*hinking about God broadens your vision. David said, "I remember the days of old. I ponder all your great works. I think about what you have done" (Psalm 143:5 NLT). Your thoughts about God will open your heart to God. The landscape of your soul becomes a vista of beauty and inspiration. David knew this truth and made meditation a constant practice.

Christian meditation is a lost art among Christians today. When we speak of Christian meditation we are not talking about the Eastern form, clearing your mind of all thoughts. Christian meditation is biblical. J.I. Packer points out that Christian meditation is an activity of holy thought, dwells on the works, ways, purposes, and promises of God, and is accomplished with the help of God. It is communion with God, and it impacts one's mind and heart.[1]

MEDITATE ON GOD'S WORD

Psalm 1:2 says that the blessed man meditates on God's law day and night. One of the best preparations of heart in quiet time is meditating on the Word of God. The Word of God is "living and active and sharper than any two-edged sword, and piercing as far as the division of soul and spirit, of both joints and marrow, and able to judge the thoughts and intentions of the heart" (Hebrews 4:12). The Word is "inspired by God and profitable for teaching, for reproof, for correction, for training in righteousness; so that the man of God may be adequate, equipped for every good work" (2 Timothy 3:16). God Himself is always present and standing behind His Word.

The book of Psalms, as the prayers and hymnbook of the Bible, is a good place to meditate for preparation of heart. Ray Stedman calls the Psalms the book of human emotions. Martin Luther loved the Psalms and used them as his daily prayer book when he was a monk. We would do well to make the Psalms our prayer book for a wonderful expression of our soul lifting itself up to the Lord.

Meditating on a psalm is my favorite way to begin my quiet time. I like to read at least one psalm each day. In fact, I often say that a psalm a day will keep the devil away. How will you know which psalm to read? You may choose to start at Psalm 1 and continue on each day until you read Psalm 150. In fact, if you do this and then add the book of Proverbs, you can read through Psalms and Proverbs twice in a year. If this idea is appealing to you, try using the Psalms/Proverbs reading guide included in *The Quiet Time Notebook*. Some mornings you may just choose to meditate on a favorite psalm. God has used many psalms in a powerful way in my life. These include Psalms 1, 5, 18, 25, 31, 34, 37, 63, 73, and 139, all with special, life-changing phrases and verses. God will give you favorites as you study Psalms and Proverbs.

When you meditate on God's Word, you take it in slowly and think long and hard about its meaning. You ask the question, what is God saying in this passage of Scripture? Your journal can be a great help as you learn to meditate on Scripture. Read a psalm and write a significant verse or phrase in your journal. Then write out why it is significant to you today, what God seems to be saying in the verse, and how it makes a difference to you in your own life. For example, one day I read Psalm 103, a psalm of David, to prepare my heart. This is what I wrote in my journal:

> "Bless the LORD, O my soul" (Psalm 103:1). What did David mean when he said that? The word is *barakh* and means "to kneel down, to bend the knee, to praise." It is a benevolent greeting from one person to another. This is a call to praise that David gives to himself, perhaps to shake off apathy or gloom, using his mind and memory to kindle his emotions (commentary on the psalms by Derek Kidner). If I could have the heart of anyone, it would be the heart of David. I want to be a woman after God's own heart. It seems he has composed a hymn in Psalm 103 to help the people of God remember some of the benefits from the Lord in order to chase away apathy, gloom, self-pity, sadness. I would do well to think about God's benefits in my own life and how He has dealt bountifully with me.

Notice I also included a quote from a commentary in my journal. Because I spend so much time in the Psalms, I have collected many commentaries on them. Now I have the benefit of seeing what others have said about some of my favorite verses in the Psalms.

You can meditate on God's Word throughout the day as a verse impacts your mind and heart. I have been thinking about some passages of Scripture for years. Often those passages of Scripture have formed the basis of a message series or a book of quiet times.

Have you ever studied a painting? Henri Nouwen wrote a book entitled *The Return of the Prodigal Son* after observing and meditating on the painting of the same name by Rembrandt. His book is an example of what can happen when you take time to think long and hard about something with much treasure hidden in it. Meditation helps you dig for that treasure. It takes time to see all the gold come to light. The same is true with God's Word. Time spent thinking about what it says will yield blessed life-transforming nuggets of truth.

Transformation occurs in your life as the Holy Spirit applies God's Word to your heart. Paul told the Corinthian church that "we all, with unveiled face, beholding as in a mirror the glory of the Lord, are being transformed into the same image from glory to glory, just as from the Lord, the Spirit" (2 Corinthians 3:18). The mirror is the Word of God (James 1:23-35). The Lord will use it to change your life. That is why meditating on God's Word is such a powerful preparation of heart. Try to find a way to begin your quiet time with God's Word, especially in the Psalms.

MEDITATE WITH MUSIC

Music is the language of the heart. It is the one gift the Lord has given us that has the power to soothe a wounded heart. Its effectiveness is especially seen in the times when all hope seems lost. You may be in such pain that opening your journal or Bible may be nearly impossible. Those are the times when God can use music to open your heart so that you will be able to hear His Word. The Bible urges us to "sing praises to the Lord" (Psalm 68:32). Paul encourages us in Ephesians to "sing and make melody with your heart to the Lord" (Ephesians 5:19).

- "Music is the foretaste of eternal life" (unknown).

- "Where words fail, music speaks" (Hans Christian Anderson).

- "After silence, that which comes nearest to expressing the inexpressible is music" (Aldous Huxley).

- "Music is the divine way to tell beautiful, poetic things to the heart" (Pablo Casals).

- "Music washes away from the soul the dust of everyday life" (Berthold Auerbach).

- "Without music, life is a journey through the desert" (Pat Conroy).

Music lifts the spirit, fills the soul, and impacts the mind, emotions, and will.

How can you add music to your quiet time? First, meditate on hymns from a good hymnbook. A.W. Tozer loved hymns and had a collection of old hymnals. He said that "after the Bible, the next most valuable book is a good hymnal. Let any new Christian spend a year prayerfully meditating on the hymns of Watts and Wesley alone, and he or she will become a fine theologian."[2] The hymnal I love is *Hymns for the Family of God*. It has a permanent place in my quiet time basket. I don't use it every day, but occasionally I will pull it out and start singing many of my favorite hymns such as "How Great Thou Art," "Great Is Thy Faithfulness," "To God Be the Glory," "And Can It Be," and "My Jesus, I Love Thee." Try singing a whole group of hymns to the Lord. It will lift your heart to the Lord. If you don't know the melodies of some of the great hymns and you have access to the Internet, go to www.hymnsite.com or www.cyberhymnal.org. These websites play the music of these hymns, and you can sing to your heart's delight. Instead of a hymnbook, you might choose a songbook of some of the current worship choruses such as "In His Time," "Lord, I Lift Your Name on High," or "Shout to the Lord." Some of the best worship songbooks are by Integrity's Hosanna! Music. Finally, if singing a tune is not your gift, you may simply read the hymns or worship songs out loud as poetry.

Another way to add music to your quiet time is through worship music on audiotapes or compact discs. One of my permanent quiet time resources in my basket is a small compact disc player with headphones. Sometimes I will just put on a CD of worship music, close my eyes, and meditate on the words, allowing the music to calm my spirit and set my thoughts and heart on the Lord. Some of my favorite worship CDs are by Hillsong Music Australia, Integrity Music, and Johnny Mann *(Glorify His Name in Quiet Time)*. I also love to listen to CDs by Stefanie Kelly, Mary Naman, Kathy Troccoli, Twila Paris, Steve Green, Steven Curtis Chapman, and Kelly Willard. Sometimes I will put on a CD as background music for my quiet time.

Oh, how wonderful it is to meditate on the words of a wonderful piece of music. God will often use it to turn your eyes to Him.

Read the following hymn, "My Jesus, I Love Thee" (by William R. Featherston), and notice how powerful the effect can be on your quiet time, even without the music.

My Jesus, I love Thee, I know Thou art mine;
For Thee all the follies of sin I resign.
My gracious Redeemer, my Savior art Thou;
If ever I loved Thee, my Jesus, 'tis now.

I love Thee because Thou hast first loved me,
And purchased my pardon on Calvary's tree.
I love Thee for wearing the thorns on Thy brow;
If ever I loved Thee, my Jesus 'tis now.

I'll love Thee in life, I will love Thee in death,
And praise Thee as long as Thou lendest me breath;
And say when the death dew lies cold on my brow:
If ever I loved Thee, my Jesus 'tis now.

In mansions of glory and endless delight,
I'll ever adore Thee in heaven so bright;
I'll sing with the glittering crown on my brow:
If ever I loved Thee, my Jesus 'tis now.

MEDITATE WITH DEVOTIONAL BOOKS

Who you read becomes the example you follow. And who you follow determines who you become. The writer of Hebrews encourages us to "Remember those who led you, who spoke the word of God to you; and considering the result of their conduct, imitate their faith" (Hebrews 13:7). Godly men and women who have gone before us can serve as our most powerful mentors in life. Their books can become timely influences to shape our spiritual life. As the writer of Ecclesiastes says, "The words of the wise prod us to live well. They're like nails hammered home, holding life together. They are given by God, the one Shepherd" (Ecclesiastes 12:11 MSG).

The words of committed men and women of God in books they have written also serve as a powerful preparation of heart. These men and women had hearts that were open to God and dared to draw near to Him. Ecclesiastes 12:11 is an encouragement to include good devotional books in your quiet time with God. In choosing books to prepare my heart, I look for authors who are wise, who have hearts with a highway to heaven, who speak the Word of God, and who have a faith that may be imitated. Choose the Christian classics—devotional books that have stood the test of time and are true to God's Word. These authors always use the Bible as the authority for their beliefs. Books of opinions and nice thoughts are fluff compared to the deeper devotional classics. In fact, some popular books in bookstores may claim to be spiritual, but often they have very little to do with knowing God. Some have no mention of God at all and focus on an inner strength apart from anything to do with God. Some of the best authors are A.W. Tozer, Oswald Chambers, Hannah Whitall Smith, Andrew Murray, R.A. Torrey, Amy Carmichael, F.B. Meyer, Charles Haddon Spurgeon, Alan Redpath, E.M. Bounds, Mrs. Charles Cowman, and J.I. Packer.

How should you use classic devotional books in your quiet time? It will depend on the layout of the book. Some devotional books are organized according to the 365 days of the year. Examples of these books are *My Utmost for His Highest* by Oswald Chambers, *Streams in the Desert* by Mrs. Charles Cowman, *Daily Light on the Daily Path* compiled by Samuel Ragster, and *God's Best Secrets* by Andrew Murray. Other books are divided according to chapters. Examples of these kinds of books are *The Pursuit of God* by A.W. Tozer, *Knowing God* by J.I. Packer, and *The God of All Comfort* by Hannah Whitall Smith. Read these latter books a chapter at a time, a page at a time, a section at a time, or even a paragraph at a time, depending on length and material depth.

Always read *devotionally* and *interactively*. William Ellery has said, "In the best books, great men talk to us, give us their most precious thoughts, and pour their souls into ours." Dialogue with authors as you read and contemplate the meaning and relevance of what they say for your own walk with God. Ask, *What do I learn about God and how to relate with Him?* Look for secrets to their intimacy with the Lord. What did they know about God, and how did it make a difference to them? When you discover something important in your reading, write it in your journal. Then, respond to what the author has said. When you read this way, the principles will go deep into your heart.

Often, the author of a devotional book will talk about a specific passage of Scripture. Look up that passage in the Bible and meditate on it. Some of the most important verses that God uses in your life will come from your devotional reading.

I like to keep a good collection of devotional books in my quiet time area. Sometimes I read from more than one devotional book. I do not always read from the same one every day. Adding a new devotional book to your collection is always exciting. I have been collecting these books for years and have a whole bookcase of devotional classics (see appendix 4 for suggested devotional reading). It will take more than a lifetime to glean all the profound truths and meditate on all the words from these hearts that have drawn near to God.

My Response

DATE:

KEY VERSE: "The words of wise men are like goads, and masters of these collections are like well-driven nails; they are given by one Shepherd" (Ecclesiastes 12:11).

FOR FURTHER THOUGHT: What is a verse you have been thinking about lately? Write it out in the space below. How can you add music to your quiet time? What books have had the most influence in your life? Who are your favorite authors? Take some time now and think about some books that you would like to read in this next year.

MY RESPONSE:

Day Twelve

QUIET TIME— WEEK TWO: BEGIN THE CLIMB

This book of the law shall not depart from
your mouth, but you shall meditate on it
day and night, so that you may be careful
to do according to all that is written
in it; for then you will make your way
prosperous, and then you will have success.

JOSHUA 1:8

PREPARE YOUR HEART

Robert Murray McCheyne was a young Scottish pastor who lived for only 30 years on this earth. The Lord gave him a brief life, yet McCheyne's life has influenced thousands down through the years as a result of his writings, published in the *Memoirs and Remains of Robert Murray McCheyne* by Andrew Bonar. McCheyne had such an intimate relationship with the Lord that when people were around him, they wanted to know God. What was McCheyne's secret? It was his quiet time with the Lord. Andrew Bonar describes it like this:

> The details of the manner of McCheyne's life, and of the way he conducted himself as a minister of the gospel, have for a hundred years been studied by other Christian workers who have longed to see God's blessing resting upon them as it rested richly upon every part of the service of this young man of God. He resolutely secured time for devotion before breakfast each day, believing that three chapters from the Bible were little enough food for his soul at the beginning of each day. He refused to give to his people on the Lord's day anything which had not cost him much of diligent application in study, meditation, and prayer. When asked by a friend about his view of how one should prepare for the pulpit, he called attention to Exodus 27:20: "Beaten oil—beaten oil for the lamps of the sanctuary." He greatly admired the words of Jeremy Taylor: "If thou meanest to enlarge thy religion, do it rather by enlarging thine ordinary devotions than thy extraordinary." While McCheyne did set apart special seasons for prayer and fasting, the real secret of his soul's prosperity lay in the daily enlargement of his own heart in fellowship with God. On one Sunday his diary carried the comments, "Very happy in my work. Too little prayer in the morning. Must try to get early to bed on Saturday, that I may 'rise a great while before day.'"[1]

Do you have the same resolve and conviction that Robert Murray McCheyne had, that you won't give others anything that does not cost you much in diligent application in study, meditation, and prayer? Thinking about these things challenges the heart, but the possible influence you will have for the Lord on the thousands around you is well worth the price.

Take some time now and think about the words of Psalm 1. Write any insights below.

Read and Study God's Word

1. You can find great value in meditating on the Word of God. God called Joshua to accomplish a great task—to take His people into the promised land. He was following in the footsteps of Moses, the man of God. What a daunting task! And yet God called him to do it. He gave him some words of instruction that would help him in this great work. Read Joshua 1:6-9 and record what you learn from these verses.

2. What is the great value of meditation according to the Word of God in Joshua 1:8?

3. Look at the following verses and record what you learn about meditation:

   Psalm 63:6-8

   Psalm 77:6,12

   Psalm 119:15,27,148

Adore God in Prayer

Will you turn to Psalm 63 and pray these words to the Lord today? Underline those verses that impress your heart and think about them throughout the day.

Yield Yourself to God

There are times when solitude is better than society, and silence is wiser than speech. We should be better Christians if we were more alone, waiting upon God, and gathering through meditation on his Word spiritual strength for labour in his service. We ought to muse upon the things of God, because we thus get the real nutriment out of them. Truth is something like the cluster of the vine: if we would have wine from it, we must bruise it; we must press and squeeze it many times. The bruiser's feet must come down joyfully upon the bunches, or else the juice will not flow; and they must well tread the grapes, or else much of the precious liquid will be wasted. So we must, by meditation, tread the clusters of truth, if we would get the wine of consolation there from. Our bodies are not supported by merely taking food into the mouth, but the process which really supplies the muscle, and the nerve, and the sinew, and the bone, is the process of digestion. It is by digestion that the outward food becomes assimilated with the inner life. Our souls are not nourished merely by listening awhile to this, and then to that, and then to the other part of divine truth. Hearing, reading, marking, and learning, all require inwardly digesting to complete their usefulness, and the inward digesting of the truth lies for the most part in meditating upon it. Why is it that some Christians, although they hear many sermons, make but slow advances in the divine life? Because they neglect their closets, and do not thoughtfully meditate on God's Word. They love the wheat, but they do not grind it; they would have the corn, but they will not go forth into the fields to gather it; the fruit hangs upon the tree, but they will not pluck it; the water flows at their feet, but they will not stoop to drink it. From such folly deliver us, O Lord, and be this our resolve this morning, "I will meditate in thy precepts."[2]

> Charles Haddon Spurgeon
> *Morning and Evening*

Enjoy His Presence

Think about the value of meditating on God's Word. Will you take time, day by day, to live in God's Word and think about every word, every phrase, every verse? Write a prayer, expressing all that is on your heart, in the space provided.

Rest in His Love

"My eyes anticipate the night watches, that I may meditate on Your word" (Psalm 119:148).

Notes—Week Two

Week Three

EXPLORE THE LANDSCAPE

Days 13-18

Day Thirteen

SECRET TWO:
READ AND STUDY
GOD'S WORD

Your word is truth.

JOHN 17:17

∞

You can know what is true. Why? Because God has spoken. When Jesus prayed, He said, "Your word is truth" (John 17:17). One of the greatest gifts we have been given is the Bible, God's Word. What you do with God's Word will determine the depth of your radical intimacy with Him.

One morning as I began my quiet time in the first chapter of Luke, I became overwhelmed with the difficulties in my life. At that very moment, the light from the sunrise glimmered with such intensity through the windows that it prompted me to write a prayer in my journal: "Lord, I need a sunrise in my life." Then I turned to Luke 1:67-79, the prophecy of Zacharias talking about John the Baptist and the coming Messiah. My heart jumped when I read verses 78-79: "The Sunrise from on high will visit us, to shine upon those who sit in darkness and the shadow of death, to guide our feet into the way of peace." I thought, *Only God, in the whole universe, could cause the sun to rise in a certain way, prompt me to write a prayer for a sunrise, and then show me a new name for Jesus and reveal something new about His character to me.* That is the power of God and His Word.

The Bible has become a friend to me, for it leads me to Jesus. I can trace my experience with Him through so many of the words found on its pages. During a difficult time, the Lord encouraged me with Psalm 31:7-8: "Because You have seen my affliction; You have known the troubles of my soul, and You have not given me over into the hand of the enemy; You have set my feet in a large place." During a time of anxiety He took me to Philippians 4:6-7: "Be anxious for nothing, but in everything by prayer and supplication let your requests be made known to God. And the peace of God, which surpasses all comprehension, will guard your hearts and your minds in Christ Jesus." During a decision about ministry, God took me to Ephesians 5:15-16: "Therefore be careful how you walk, not as unwise men, but as wise, making the most of your time, because the days are evil. So then do not be foolish, but understand what the will of the Lord is."

Living in the Word of God is a priority for every child of God who would be a radical disciple of Jesus Christ. I want to challenge you to go beyond the portals of this world and commit yourself to the study of God's Word. I want you to be like the Bereans in Paul's day described in Acts 17:11 (NIV): "The Bereans were of more noble character than the Thessalonians, for they received the message with great eagerness and examined the Scriptures every day to see if what Paul said was true." I want you to be like Mary, who sat at the Lord's feet, listening to Him speak (Luke 10:39). Rather than being distracted and pulled in many directions (the Greek word is *perispao)* like Martha, become a *mathetes* like Mary, a disciple of Jesus, one who learns and adopts the philosophy, practices, and way of life of the Teacher. Will you dedicate yourself to be a disciple of Christ who has the priority of sitting at the Lord's feet and listening to His Word?

The Great Value of God's Word

Why is God's Word so important? First, because it is *inspired by God*. Second Peter 1:20-21 (NIV) says that "no prophecy of Scripture came about by the prophet's own interpretation. For prophecy never had its origin in the will of man, but men spoke from God as they were carried along by the Holy Spirit." Paul tells us in 2 Timothy 3:16 (NIV) that "all Scripture is God-breathed." Because Scripture is inspired by God, it reveals God to us. It is the very thoughts and words of God. Therefore, we can know God and His perspective. The Bible has often been likened to God's love letter to us.

Second, God's Word is important because it is *truth*. Jesus said in John 17:17, "Your word is truth." That means it is accurate, reliable, and dependable. You can believe what it says. In a world with many lies and deceptions, you can go to one place to find out what is true—the Word of God. In fact, it is more true than your feelings and circumstances.

Third, the Bible is important because it is *authoritative*. It possesses the supreme right to command your beliefs and your actions. The writer of Hebrews tells us "it judges the thoughts and attitudes of the heart" (4:12 NIV). It is the "lamp for [our] feet" and the "light for [our] path" (Psalm 119:105 NLT). Paul says that the Word is "profitable for teaching, for reproof, for correction, for training in righteousness; so that the man of God may be adequate, equipped for every good work" (2 Timothy 3:16-17).

Finally, the fourth reason why God's Word is so important in your life is that *it accomplishes God's purpose in our lives*. God says in Isaiah 55:10-11 (NIV), "As the rain and snow come down from heaven, and do not return to it without watering the earth and making it bud and flourish, so that it yields seed for the sower and bread for the eater, so is my word that goes out from my mouth: it will not return to me empty, but will accomplish what I desire and achieve the purpose for which I sent it." God, through His Holy Spirit, opens our eyes to the meaning of His Word and uses it to lead us in life. Without the Holy Spirit, the Bible would be just words on a page. Because the Bible is a living book, it transforms us and makes us adequate for every good work. That means that God equips us for everything He asks of us.

One day, a man set sail from the coast of Massachusetts. After some time, thick fog blanketed the water, reducing visibility to zero. One wrong move and his tiny craft would be crushed like paper by the commercial vessels using the same passage of water. Describing his experience, the man said, "It was as though the windows were painted black, there was zero visibility, and we were forced to fly by instruments only." Sometimes in your life the windows seem to be painted black, the visibility is zero, and you are forced to fly by instruments only. Your radar is the Word of God. As you read and study God's Word, He will guide you into the path of life and truth.

My Response

DATE:

KEY VERSE: "For the word of God is full of living power. It is sharper than the sharpest knife, cutting deep into our innermost thoughts and desires" (Hebrews 4:12 NLT).

FOR FURTHER THOUGHT: Have you chosen the first priority of a disciple, to sit at the feet of the Lord and listen to His Word?

MY RESPONSE:

Day Fourteen

YOUR BIBLE READING PLAN

Let the word of Christ richly dwell within you.

COLOSSIANS 3:16

∽

lan to be in God's Word every day. Paul said, "Let the word of Christ richly dwell within you" (Colossians 3:16). The word "richly" is *plousios* in the Greek and means "extravagant." Extravagance in God's Word is the norm in God's economy. Enter into this extravagance by choosing a formal Bible reading plan.

- *A devotional Bible*—A devotional Bible gives you a defined portion of Scripture to read each day, eliminating the decision about what and how much to read. *The NIV Men's* or *Women's Devotional Bible* (Zondervan) offers a yearly Bible reading plan and includes daily devotional readings. *The One Year Bible* (Tyndale House Publishers, available in

NIV, NASB, NLT, KJV, and NKJV), a favorite of mine, offers a daily portion of Scripture from the Old Testament, the New Testament, Psalms, and Proverbs. *The Daily Bible* (Harvest House Publishers) offers a yearly, chronological Bible reading plan with brief introductions providing context for your study.

- *A devotional reading guide*—My favorite guides are *The Daily Walk* and *A Closer Walk* by Walk Through the Bible Ministries (www.walkthru.org), *In Touch Magazine* by Charles Stanley's In Touch Ministries (www.intouch.org), and *Tabletalk* by R.C. Sproul's Ligonier Ministries (www.ligonier.org).

- *The Bible in a year*—Simply reading through four or five chapters each day will take you through the Bible in a year.

- *A psalm and a proverb a day*—This plan will take you through Psalms and Proverbs twice in a year.

- *A passage or a chapter a day*—Choose a book of the Bible and read a passage each day until you complete that entire book. Most Bibles organize passages within chapters by theme, such as "The Temptation of Jesus" in Matthew 4:1-11 (NASB) or "Parables on Prayer" in Luke 18:1-8 (NASB).

- *A comprehensive Bible study*—Bible studies by Quiet Time Ministries Press, NavPress, Precept Ministries International, Living Proof Ministries, Bible Study Fellowship, and Community Bible Study will take you to God's Word each day and help you dig for treasure you might not find as easily on your own. The quiet time studies *Pilgrimage of the Heart, Revive My Heart!,* and *A Heart That Dances,* published by NavPress, and *A Heart on Fire* and *A Heart to See Forever* published by Quiet Time Ministries Press, are organized according to the P.R.A.Y.E.R. Quiet Time Plan, giving you a rich, comprehensive quiet time with the Lord every day.

Ask God for wisdom when choosing a reading plan for the year. You may even want to go to a Christian bookstore to examine the different daily devotional Bibles and other materials mentioned. Don't be afraid to change your Bible reading plan from year to year. This will keep your quiet time exciting and vibrant. Selecting a definite Bible reading plan will encourage consistency in your quiet time. Once you have chosen your Bible reading plan, it's time to dig into the Word of God!

My Response

DATE:

KEY VERSE: "All Scripture is inspired by God and is useful to teach us what is true and to make us realize what is wrong in our lives. It straightens us out and teaches us to do what is right. It is God's way of preparing us in every way, fully equipped for every good thing God wants us to do" (2 Timothy 3:16-17 NLT).

FOR FURTHER THOUGHT: What will you choose as your Bible reading plan this year? Consider the amount of time you will invest each day, the plan's viewpoint, the cost, and your circle of fellowship when you make your decision.

MY RESPONSE:

DIGGING
DEEPER

*Open my eyes, that I may behold
wonderful things from Your law.*

PSALM 119:18

⸎

reasure in God's Word is discovered. There was a
time in the life of the Israelites when they "did not
incline their ear" to listen for God's voice (Jeremiah 7:24). They were
not open to discovery. The words of the psalmist encourage discovery:
"Open my eyes, that I may behold wonderful things from Your law"
(Psalm 119:18). The Bible is a place of retreat where you meet with God.
Approach His Word with the wholehearted expectation that He is going
to speak to you.

When my husband and I visited Florence, Italy, we sought out
the Medici Chapel, designed by Michelangelo. The night before our
visit, we had read about a recent discovery of some of Michelangelo's

drawings. While changing the film in my camera, I felt a tug on my arm as my husband quickly whispered into my ear, "Don't say anything… just follow me." Away from the mass of fellow tourists, a guard led us down carved steps beneath the chapel. We entered a small room where Michelangelo had slept. The walls were covered with dozens of sketches for the sculptures, architectural drawings, and even a self-portrait. The discovery of this hidden treasure took our breath away. That same joy of discovery exists when you open the Word of God.

You have your Bible and a Bible reading plan—now is the time to experience devotional study. The Greek word for *devote* is *prokarteo* and means "to tarry, remain somewhere, or remain long with the thought." We want to tarry awhile in the Word of God. Merrill C. Tenney says, "Devotional study impresses the message on a believing heart. The crown of all study is devotional study. Devotional study is not so much of a technique as a spirit. It is the spirit of eagerness which seeks the mind of God; it is the spirit of humility which listens readily to the voice of God; it is the spirit of adventure which pursues earnestly the will of God; it is the spirit of adoration which rests in the presence of God."[1] In devotional Bible study, you explore a passage of Scripture to discover all that is in it. What follows is a simple way to study any passage of Scripture devotionally. You may not necessarily use all the techniques every day. Be creative.

ONE SIGNIFICANT OBSERVATION

Read your selected Scripture slowly and carefully, thinking about all you see in the passage. What impresses you most about this passage? Is a word, a verse, or a phrase significant to you? Does a person, event, or action stand out to you? Does a thought or emotion leap from the page? Does this passage illustrate a particular characteristic of God? Ask God to speak to you. Then, write your one significant observation in your journal or in the first section on the "Read and Study God's Word" page in *The Quiet Time Notebook* (See Figure 5 on page 128). For example, let's say you are reading James 1:1-3. You might choose the following significant observation: "The testing of my faith produces endurance." It can be obvious and simple, or creative, deep, and profound.

Immediate Context

As you think about your one significant observation, ask yourself what is going on in and around this chapter. What is the main focus? Place yourself in the environment of the passage. Dallas Willard says, "We must prayerfully, but boldly use our God-given imaginations to fill out the reality of events in terms of what it would be like if we were Moses standing by the bush, little Samuel lying in his darkened room, Elisha under inspiration from the minstrel, Ananias receiving his vision about Paul, or Peter on his rooftop."[2] Always ask, what is the subject of the passage? For example, if you are reading Hebrews 11, the immediate context is faith. In John 10, the chapter is all about Jesus as the good Shepherd. Isaiah 53 focuses on the Suffering Servant. In Genesis 1, God is creating the heavens and the earth. Revelation 19 is all about the return of Jesus Christ. In James 1:1-3, the immediate context is the value of trials.

Insights, Word Meanings, and Cross-References

Choose one of the following methods to dig deeper into the Word of God, depending on your time, study tools, and interest.

Record your insights. From your one significant observation, ask questions like these: Why do I like this phrase so much? What do I see in that short phrase? What does it mean? How will it help me in my life? For example, from your one significant observation, "The testing of your faith produces endurance" (James 1:1-3), you may observe that trials are tests of faith and testing is productive. Write those insights in your journal or under the Insights/Word Meanings/Cross-References section on the "Read and Study God's Word" page of your *Quiet Time Notebook*.

Look up word meanings. To understand the meaning of a word, choose a key word, look up its meaning in a concordance, and write what you learn in your journal or under the Insights/Word Meanings/Cross-References section on the "Read and Study God's Word" page of your *Quiet Time Notebook*. In your one significant observation, "the testing of your faith produces endurance" in James 1:3, a key word is "endurance." A key word is repeated in the passage or essential to the text. Exhaustive concordances are available for most translations of the

Bible. Purchase the exhaustive concordance for the translation you use in your quiet time.

How to Use Your Concordance

Step 1—Find the key word in your concordance. Every word in the Bible is listed in alphabetical order in an exhaustive (complete) concordance.

ENDURANCE		
your *e* you will gain your lives.	Lk 21:19	*5281*
as servants of God, in much *e*,	2Co 6:4	*5281*
For you have need of *e*,	Heb 10:36	*5281*
and let us run with *e* the race	Heb 12:1	*5281*
testing of your faith produces *e*.	* Jas 1:3	* *5281*
And let *e* have *its* perfect result,	Jas 1:4	*5281*
You have heard of the *e* of Job and	Jas 5:11	*5281*

Figure 2. New American Standard Exhaustive Concordance.

Step 2—Find your Scripture verse. Locate your Scripture verse under that key word. For example, once you find *endurance* in the NASB concordance (*patience* in the KJV Strong's concordance), locate James 1:3.

Step 3—Write down the Strong's number, located to the right of that verse. The Strong's number for *endurance* (*patience* in KJV) in James 1:3 is 5281.

Step 4—Locate the Strong's number and word definition in either the Hebrew (Old Testament) or Greek (New Testament) dictionary in the back of the concordance. In the case of *endurance* in James 1:3, Strong's number 5281 yields the definition for endurance of "a remaining behind, a patient enduring."

5281. ὑπομονή hupomonē; from *5278; a remaining behind, a patient enduring:*—endurance(7), enduring(1), patient(1), perseverance (21), steadfastness(3).

Figure 3. Greek dictionary in the
New American Standard Exhaustive Concordance.

Look up cross-references. The purpose of a cross-reference is to take into account the whole counsel of God's Word, clarifying the meaning of the text. When you cross-reference a verse, you look for other verses in the Bible related topically to the selected Scripture you are studying. This may or may not flow from your one significant observation but may be another phrase that intrigues you. To accomplish this kind of study, you need a Bible with cross-references, that is, verse references printed in the side or center margins.

How to Cross-Reference a Verse

Step 1—Select a favorite phrase.

Step 2—In a cross-reference Bible, find the letter of the alphabet at the beginning of the selected phrase.

Step 3—Find the verse number in the margin and the letter of the alphabet following that number. Next to the letter will be one or more verse cross-references.

Step 4—Write down the cross-reference verse in the Insights/ Word Meanings/Cross-References section on the "Read and Study God's Word" page of your *Quiet Time Notebook.* Look up each cross-reference in your Bible and write out your insights.

Testing Your Faith

1 ¹ᵃJames, a ᵇbond-servant of God and ᶜof the Lord Jesus Christ,

¶ To ᵈthe twelve tribes who are ²ᵉdispersed abroad: ᶠGreetings.

2 ¶ ᵃConsider it all joy, my brethren, when you encounter ᵇvarious ¹trials,

3 knowing that ᵃthe testing of your ᵇfaith produces ¹ᶜendurance.

4 And let ¹ᵃendurance have *its* perfect ²result, so that you may be ³ᵇperfect and complete, lacking in nothing.

1:1 ¹Or *Jacob* ²Lit *in the Dispersion* ᵃActs 12:17 ᵇTitus 1:1 ᶜRom 1:1 ᵈLuke 22:30 ᵉJohn 7:35 ᶠActs 15:23
2 ¹Or *temptations* ᵃMatt 5:12; James 1:12 ᵇ1 Pet 1:6
3 ¹Or *steadfastness* ᵃ1 Pet 1:7◄ ᵇHeb 6:12 ᶜLuke 21:19
4 ¹V 3, note 1 ²Lit *work* ³Or *mature* ᵃLuke 21:19 ᵇMatt 5:48; Col 4:12

Figure 4. An excerpt from a cross-reference Bible.

For example, if you were to cross-reference "the testing of your faith produces endurance" in James 1:1-3, one of the cross-references is 1 Peter 1:7. This cross-reference amplifies the testing of faith, that it is more valuable than gold and will result in praise, glory, and honor at the revelation of Christ. A series of cross-reference insights becomes a reference study (See Figures 6a and 6b on pages 129–130.) Two good cross-reference Bible study tools are *The Treasury of Scripture Knowledge* and *Nave's Topical Bible*.

SUMMARY AND CONCLUSIONS

Write a one- or two-sentence summary based on your study that will help you remember God's truth.

APPLICATION IN MY LIFE

In application, allow the truth of God's Word to infiltrate your life and determine how you live. Ask God to make His Word live in you, transform you, and make you more like Jesus. The following questions are helpful when applying God's Word to your life:

- How does what you have learned give you God's view of your present situation in life?

- What do you learn about God and His ways that may be applied to your life?

- Does God want you to obey Him in some way?

- Are you convicted of a sin that requires confession and repentance?

- How has God met your needs and present circumstances in life today?

- Do you see an example to follow in your own life?

- Does a doctrinal or ethical truth command your belief and require a change in your behavior?

- Have you discovered a life-changing verse that requires memorization?

- Did you learn anything affecting your goals in life, giving you new meaning and purpose?

- Could you encourage someone in your life with a letter, book, or phone call?

- Does someone in your life need an expression of God's love, the message of the gospel, or a need met today?

Read And Study God's Word

"Study this book of the Law continually.
Meditate on it day and night..." Joshua 1:8 NLT

Date: *Jan 21, 2005* Today's Scripture: *James 1:1-3*

Read God's Word and record One Significant Observation:

the testing of my faith produces endurance

Immediate Context:

this passage is all about trials

Insights/Word Meanings/Cross-References:

Insight: trials can be productive

Endurance - 5281 - hupomone - the quality that does not surrender under circumstances or succumb under trial

1 Peter 1:6-7 the proof of my faith is more precious than gold and will result in praise and glory at the revelation of Christ

Summary and Conclusions:

It is possible to have joy in trials. A trial makes me stronger so that I won't surrender to adverse circumstances.

Application In My Life:

This gives me the strength to stand strong in the current trial. Lord, help me see your perspective in the difficult circumstances of life.

Figure 5. "Read and Study" page from *The Quiet Time Notebook*.

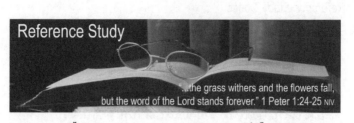

Verse/Topic:: *things not seen* Scripture: *Hebrews 11:1*

Record observations and insights from the following references related to the selected verse or topic. Define any key words.

Key Word Definitions:
Faith - confidence in divine truth (taken from the Hebrew-Greek Word Study Bible)

Romans 8:24
—————————————
Reference
Our hope is in things we cannot see at the present time. Hope is part of what it means to live by faith.

2 Corinthians 4:18
—————————————
Reference
These things not seen are eternal. Faith is how we keep our eyes fixed on the eternal.

2 Corinthians 5:7
—————————————
Reference
We are to walk by faith not by sight.

Hebrews 11:7
—————————————
Reference
God warned Noah about things not seen — Noah's faith translated into action. He built an ark.

Figure 6a. "Reference Study" page 1 from *The Quiet Time Notebook.*

Hebrews 11:27

Reference

Moses was able to leave Egypt, not fear, and endure, because he saw Him who is unseen. Faith is the way to see what is not seen.

Colossians 1:15

Reference

God is invisible yet we can "see" Him by faith. How much we "see" is displayed in our actions and life.

Hebrews 11:13

Reference

Faith means we see God's promises from a distance and welcome them. Our life then lines up with what we have seen in God's promises.

John 8:56

Reference

Abraham's faith in the future coming of Jesus resulted in joy and gladness.

Summary and Conclusions:

1. God's promises are those "things not seen." 2. I am to look at God's promises and welcome them into my life. 3. I am to conduct my life by God's promises. 4. My faith results in hope, joy, gladness. 5. I may die in faith, not receiving the promise until heaven.

Application In My Life:

It is my preoccupation with God's promises from the Word of God that is going to make the difference in having a life pleasing to God. I must live in the Word to know and understand His promises.

Figure 6b. "Reference Study" page 2 from *The Quiet Time Notebook*.

My Response

DATE:

KEY VERSE: "Be diligent to present yourself approved to God as a workman who does not need to be ashamed, accurately handling the word of truth" (2 Timothy 2:15).

FOR FURTHER THOUGHT: What is the most important idea you learned that you can apply in your quiet time as you study God's Word?

MY RESPONSE:

Day Sixteen

GET PERSONAL

All Scripture is inspired by God and is useful to teach us what is true and to make us realize what is wrong in our lives.

2 TIMOTHY 3:16 NLT

⁓⧓

The Bible is written for you; it is God's love letter to you. When this truth makes its way to your heart, you will not be able to stay away from the Word of God. Paul said, "All Scripture is inspired by God and is useful to teach us what is true and to make us realize what is wrong in our lives. It straightens us out and teaches us to do what is right. It is God's way of preparing us in every way, fully equipped for every good thing God wants us to do" (2 Timothy 3:16-17 NLT).

God speaks to you, individually and directly, from His Word. One morning during a Revive My Heart! class, a woman raised her hand and asked me if she could share an experience from her study. When she came to a question about a verse in the Bible, she automatically wrote what God was saying to people *in general.* Suddenly, she realized God was not speaking to people in general; God was speaking *to her!* She rewrote her answer, beginning with "God wants me to…" She exclaimed to the class, "I have learned that God wants to speak directly to me from His Word." From that day forward, her book of quiet times became filled with the insights and observations she was discovering from God's Word.

God is with you when you are reading or studying His Word. You are never alone. The Bible is not just words on a page. Behind the written Word is the Person of God Himself. The writer of Hebrews confirms this truth: "The word of God is living and active. Sharper than any double-edged sword, it penetrates even to dividing soul and spirit, joints and marrow; it judges the thoughts and attitudes of the heart" (Hebrews 4:12 NIV). As you sit down to read and study God's Word, always remember God is there, waiting to speak to you.

God will help you interpret and apply His Word. Jesus said in John 14:26, "But the Helper, the Holy Spirit, whom the Father will send in My name, He will teach you all things, and bring to your remembrance all that I said to you." As you think about God speaking to you from His Word, examine and interpret each passage in context. The verses have one meaning and many applications. As you observe, interpret, and apply what you read, God will speak to you. He may give you more than one application from a passage of Scripture. For example, in Joshua 1:9 (NIV), God says, "Have I not commanded you? Be strong and courageous. Do not be terrified; do not be discouraged, for the LORD your God will be with you wherever you go." In context, Joshua has been given a huge task. God's expectation of him was to be strong and courageous and never give up. That is the meaning. Now how may I apply it? What tasks has God given me? One example would be that God has given me the task of leading Quiet Time Ministries. He wants me to be strong and courageous in my ministry. How will I respond? I will say, "Yes, Lord," and launch out in faith. Someone else may read Joshua 1:9 and gain confidence to stand up in front of a group and teach. Another person may be encouraged to take on a new job.

MAKE THE BIBLE YOUR OWN

Once you've chosen your everyday Bible, make it your own, personalize it, and spend time with it as you would a good friend so that it will "dwell in you richly" (Colossians 3:16 NIV).

- Always write a personal response, assuming the Word of God is written for you: "God wants *me* to do this...*I* am to do the following."

- Underline significant verses.

- Write insights beside significant verses.

- Write important dates beside significant verses.

- Explore the entire Bible, the Old Testament as well as the New, the Psalms as well as the Gospels, and Revelation as well as the letters of Paul.

- Carry your Bible with you everywhere. The devil is not afraid of a Bible that has dust on it. According to Ephesians 6, God's Word is the sword that defeats the devil, the enemy of our souls. One Bible in the hand is worth two in the bookcase.

- Live in the Word so much that the pages become worn. Get to know your friend from cover to cover.

My Response

DATE:

KEY VERSE: "Above all, you must understand that no prophecy in Scripture ever came from the prophets themselves or because they wanted to prophesy. It was the Holy Spirit who moved the prophets to speak from God" (2 Peter 1:20-21 NLT).

FOR FURTHER THOUGHT: What does it mean to personalize Scripture, and what difference will that make in your quiet time? Take some time now to personalize Psalm 34 as a prayer to the Lord. Here's an example: *I will bless You, Lord, at all times. Your praise shall continually be in my mouth. My soul will boast in You, Lord...*

MY RESPONSE:

Day Seventeen

MY FAVORITE
BIBLE STUDY TOOLS

*Be careful how you walk, not as unwise
men but as wise, making the most of
your time, because the days are evil.*

EPHESIANS 5:15-16

No time is ever wasted in God's Word. Paul encouraged the Ephesian church to "be careful how you walk, not as unwise men but as wise, making the most of your time, because the days are evil" (Ephesians 5:15-16). What is the wise choice? Time in God's Word. Peter said that "the grass withers, and the flower falls off, but the word of the Lord endures forever" (1 Peter 1:24-25). You can sit at the feet of the Lord and listen to His Word in many ways. Read from a devotional Bible, use a prepared Bible study such as *Revive My Heart*, read a Psalm and then cross-reference a verse, or read a chapter from the Gospel of John and then write a verse and insights in your journal. All

Bible study is an eternal investment in radical intimacy.

Effective Bible study tools are like surgical instruments that allow you to accurately operate on the Word of God. For more comprehensive information about how to use these and many more exciting Bible study tools in your quiet time, you may wish to get my book *Romancing the Word* (Quiet Time Ministries Press, available in spring 2006). If you are using *The Quiet Time Notebook,* you can use the "Read and Study God's Word" pages, the "Reference Study" pages, and the "Notes" pages to record your insights from the resources that follow.

1. *The Hebrew-Greek Key Word Study Bible* (NASB), edited by Spiros Zodhiates and published by AMG Publishers, contains two Greek-Hebrew dictionaries with comprehensive and insightful definitions for most of the important words in the Bible. It also parses most of the important Greek verbs, revealing their grammatical context and explanations.

This user-friendly word-study tool is available in three translations: KJV, NASB, and NIV. Zodhiates has underlined the key words in the Bible and included Strong's numbers directly in the text so you can easily look up the definitions in the two dictionaries (lexicons), including Strong's dictionary. I prefer the KJV or NASB versions rather than the NIV because these editions contain more meaningful lexicon definitions. This is a great tool for those who travel and desire a word study resource for their quiet times on the road. *Quiet Time Notebook* application: "Read and Study God's Word" page.

2. The *New American Standard Exhaustive Concordance of the Bible,* edited by Robert L. Thomas and published by Holman Bible Publishers, contains every word in the Bible listed in alphabetical order with a Hebrew and Greek dictionary to help you understand word meanings.

Choose an exhaustive concordance that corresponds with your everyday Bible translation to define words, study topics, and locate verses. This is a great tool to help you search for an essential verse when writing a sermon, message, or devotion. *Quiet Time Notebook* application: "Read and Study God's Word" page, "Reference Study" page.

3. *The New Treasury of Scripture Knowledge,* edited by Jerome H. Smith and published by Nelson Reference, lists cross-references verse by verse, keyed to each important phrase from Genesis to Revelation.

This compendium broadens and simplifies the selection of cross-references compared to those listed in the margins of your everyday Bible. This great tool helps you discover a special verse you may have never noticed. *Quiet Time Notebook* application: "Read and Study God's Word" page, "Reference Study" page.

4. *Nave's Topical Bible* by Orville J. Nave, published by Hendrickson Publishers, organizes Scripture references according to topic in alphabetical order.

Simply find the desired topic and look up all the Scripture references. Doctrinal truths come alive when studied in the context of the whole counsel of God's Word. *Quiet Time Notebook* application: "Read and Study God's Word" page, "Reference Study" page.

5. *Matthew Henry's Commentary on the Whole Bible* by Hendrickson Publishers offers Matthew Henry's insights and applications from every passage in the Bible in one volume.

Henry uses exegetical (critical analysis) methods to produce succinct chapter summaries, outlines, and detailed explanations based on the original Greek and Hebrew. This great tool probes the meaning of a text, taking you from surface knowledge to deeper wisdom. *Quiet Time Notebook* application: "Read and Study God's Word" page, "Notes" page.

6. The *New Bible Dictionary,* edited by J.D. Douglas and published by Intervarsity Press, gives background information about people, places, events, and books of the Bible.

Encyclopedic in design, this dictionary animates the historical context for topics and themes in the Bible. This great tool transforms Scriptural passages to live theater. *Quiet Time Notebook* application: "Read and Study God's Word" page, "Notes" page.

7. *Zondervan NASB Study Bible,* edited by Kenneth Barker, features study notes keyed to Bible verses, introductions to books of the Bible,

text notes, a cross-reference system, parallel passages, a concordance, charts, maps, essays, and comprehensive indexes.

Traditional evangelical theology is presented in a comprehensive format. This is my everyday Bible: I live in it. *Quiet Time Notebook* application: "Read and Study God's Word" page, "Notes" page.

8. Audio and video tapes, CDs, periodicals, books, and sermons by well-known authors and speakers such as Charles Stanley (www.intouch.org) and R.C. Sproul (www.ligonier.org) make perfect companions for a personal spiritual retreat. Read magazines including *Leadership, Discipleship Journal, Pray!, Weavings, Christian History,* and *Christianity Today. Quiet Time Notebook* application: "Notes" page.

9. *Scholar's Library* Bible computer software by Logos Research Systems (www.logos.com) features more than 250 Bible and reference titles using the Libronix digital search engine.

This computer program acts as an automated research assistant that searches and organizes vast amounts of study material. This great tool saves me thousands of hours of research time. *Quiet Time Notebook* application: "Read and Study God's Word" page, "Notes" page.

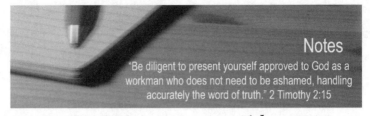

Date: *Jan 21, 2005*   Subject/Scripture: *Hebrews 11:1*

Title: *New Bible Commentary* Author/Speaker: *Peterson*

Notes:

New Bible Commentary ed. Carson, France, Motyer, Wenham (Downers Grove, IL: Inter-Varsity Press 1994), page 1346.

The writer emphasizes the similarity between OT believers and Christians today waiting for the fulfillment of God's purposes. It is a comprehensive picture of faith. Hebrews shows the relationship between faith, hope, endurance, and obedience. A faith that honors God will take God at His Word and will live in the present expectantly and obediently, waiting for Him to fulfill His promises. Faith deals with future, unseen things. The reality of what we hope for is verified in our experience when we live by faith in the promises of God. Our faith tests the invisible realities of the spiritual realm seen in God's Word such as God's existence, faithfulness to His Word, and His control over the world where we live.

Application In My Life:

How exciting a life of faith is! I can see that God wants me to be confident and expectant of Him even in my present circumstances.

Figure 7. Notes page from *The Quiet Time Notebook*

My Response

DATE:

KEY VERSE: "Study this Book of the Law continually. Meditate on it day and night so you may be sure to obey all that is written in it. Only then will you succeed" (Joshua 1:8 NLT).

FOR FURTHER THOUGHT: What Bible study tool would you like to incorporate into your quiet time?

MY RESPONSE:

Day Eighteen

QUIET TIME—
WEEK THREE:
EXPLORE THE LANDSCAPE

*All Scripture is inspired by God and is
useful to teach us what is true and to
make us realize what is wrong in our
lives. It straightens us out and teaches
us to do what is right. It is God's way of
preparing us in every way, fully equipped
for every good thing God wants us to do.*

2 TIMOTHY 3:16-17 NLT

PREPARE YOUR HEART

George Mueller spent the first 20 years of his life in deception, lying, gambling, and other indulgences. He was so steeped in a life of dishonesty that he even stole from his father, falsified accounts, and was imprisoned at the age of sixteen for stealing from a landlord. He entered the University of Halle as a divinity student because his father believed the ministry to be a reliable job for his errant son. While in school, George Mueller went with a friend to a meeting where Christians were singing hymns, reading the Bible, and praying. This was very different for Mueller, and he liked it—especially the joy he witnessed. God began to work in Mueller's heart, and he gave his life to Christ. The Lord used George Mueller in a powerful way in his lifetime. He and his wife lived out a conviction to tell no one of their needs but God alone. As a result, the Lord entrusted much to George Mueller. He developed an orphanage ministry, established the Scripture Knowledge Institution, and obtained and disbursed no less than $7,500,000 for Christian ministry.

George Mueller had a secret to his success in ministry and his relationship with the Lord. Listen to what he says:

> The first three years after conversion, I neglected the Word of God. Since I began to search it diligently, the blessing has been wonderful. I have read the Bible through one hundred times and always with increasing delight. I look upon it as a lost day when I have not a good time over the Word of God. Friends often say "I have so much to do, so many people to see, I cannot find time for Scripture study." Perhaps there are not many who have more to do than I. For more than half a century I have never known one day when I had not more business than I could get through. For forty years I have had annually about thirty thousand letters, and most of these passed through my own hands. I have nine assistants always at work corresponding in German, French, English, Danish, Italian, Russian, and other languages. Then as pastor of a church with twelve hundred believers, great has been my care. Besides, I have had charge of five immense orphanages; also, at my publishing depot, the printing and circulating of millions of tracts, books and Bibles. But I have always made it a rule never to begin work till I have had a good season with God. The vigor of our spiritual life will be in exact proportion to the place held by the Word in our life and thoughts.

The secret to George Mueller's life was time with God in His Word. Will you take some time to think about the place the Word of God has

in your own life and thoughts? Write a prayer to the Lord asking Him
to speak to you as you draw near to Him today.

READ AND STUDY GOD'S WORD

1. One person who understood the importance of the Word of
   God was the author of Psalm 119. This psalm is one of the
   pinnacles of truth about God's Word. Read Psalm 119:89-112
   and record everything you learn about God's Word.

2. Look at the following verses and write what you learn
   about the Word of God. Personalize your insights whenever
   possible. For example, "I live on every word that proceeds
   out of the mouth of God" (Matthew 4:4).

   Isaiah 55:10-11

   Matthew 4:4

2 Timothy 3:16

1 Peter 1:24-25

3. Summarize in two or three sentences what you have learned about the Word of God.

ADORE GOD IN PRAYER

Use the words of the psalmist for your prayer to the Lord today:

Teach me, O Lord, the way of Your statutes,
And I shall observe it to the end.
Give me understanding, that I may observe Your law
And keep it with all my heart.
Make me walk in the path of Your commandments,
For I delight in it.
Incline my heart to Your testimonies
And not to dishonest gain.
Turn away my eyes from looking at vanity,
And revive me in Your ways.
Establish Your word to Your servant,
As that which produces reverence for You (Psalm 119:33-38).

YIELD YOURSELF TO GOD

Believer! would you abide in Jesus, be very careful to keep His commandments. Keep them in the love of your heart.

Be not content to have them in the Bible for reference, but
have them transferred by careful study, by meditation and
by prayer, by a loving acceptance, by the Spirit's teaching,
on the fleshy tables of the heart. Be not content with the
knowledge of some of the commands, those most commonly
received among Christians, while others lie unknown and
neglected…Make Paul's prayer for the Colossians yours
for yourself and all believers, that you might be filled with
the knowledge of His will in all wisdom and spiritual
understanding…Remember that this is one of the great
elements of spiritual growth—a deeper insight into the will
of God concerning you…The progressive renewal of the
Holy Spirit leads to growing like-mindedness to Christ;
then comes a delicate power of spiritual perception—a holy
instinct—by which the soul quick of understanding in the
fear of the Lord, knows to recognize the meaning and the
application of the Lord's commands to daily life in a way
that remains hidden to the ordinary Christian. Keep them
dwelling richly within you, hide them within your heart,
and you shall taste the blessedness of the man whose delight
is in the law of the Lord, and in His law doth he meditate
day and night.[1]

Andrew Murray
Abide in Christ

I can imagine some persons asking *How can I get to be in love
with the Bible?* Well, if you will only rouse yourselves to the
study of it, and ask God's assistance, He will assuredly help
you…Read the Bible as if you were seeking for something
of value. It is a good deal better to take a single chapter and
spend a month on it, than to read the Bible at random for
a month…I have carried my Bible with me a good many
years. It is worth more to me than all the Bibles in this place,
and I will tell you why; because I have got so many passages
marked in it, and if I am called upon to speak at anytime,
I am ready. I have got these little words in the margin, and
they are a sermon to me. Whether I speak about faith, hope,
charity, assurance, or on any subject whatever, it all comes

back to me. Every child of God ought to be like a soldier, and always hold himself in readiness; but we can't be ready if we don't study the Bible. So whenever you hear a good thing just put it down, because if it's good for you it will be good for somebody else; and we should pass the coin of heaven round just as we do other current coin.[2]

D.L. Moody
The Bible Reader's Guide

ENJOY HIS PRESENCE

Have you fallen in love with the Word of God and thus grown in your love for God Himself? How is your time alone with God in His Word? Close by writing a prayer to the Lord, expressing all that is on your heart.

REST IN HIS LOVE

"Let the word of Christ dwell in you richly as you teach and admonish one another with all wisdom, and as you sing psalms, hymns and spiritual songs with gratitude in your hearts to God" (Colossians 3:16 NIV).

Notes—Week Three

REACH
THE SUMMITS

Days 19-24

Day Nineteen

SECRET THREE: ADORE GOD IN PRAYER

To You, O LORD, I lift up my soul.

PSALM 25:1

⚬∞

rayer lifts the soul to God. It reaches its height of expression in response to God's Word. The psalmist has said, "To You, O LORD, I lift up my soul" (Psalm 25:1). Lifting the soul to God is not easy when circumstances of life weigh upon the heart. The Word of God untethers the soul, freeing it to lay all burdens, desires, requests, and cares upon the heart of God. Prayer ushers you into the throne room of God. Jesus says, "But you, when you pray, go into your inner room, close your door and pray to your Father who is in secret, and your Father who sees in secret will repay you" (Matthew 6:6). This "secret" place of God is His very presence. It is the large, abundant place described by the psalmists (Psalm 18:19; 31:8; 118:5) where God sets our feet in the midst of great distress. The presence of God is where we may run at all times to find refuge. "Therefore let us draw near with confidence to the throne of grace, so that we may receive mercy and find grace to help in time of need" (Hebrews 4:16).

Prayer was the habit of Jesus' life. He *often* slipped away to the wilderness to pray (Luke 5:16). Jesus modeled prayer as a *life,* not a single act of worship. Regular times of prayer produce a firsthand experience with God, resulting in extraordinary world influence. Daily intervals of prayer result in a lifestyle of interaction with God, renew your mind, transform you, and prepare you to meet life demands. A life of prayer enables you to "prove what the will of God is, that which is good and acceptable and perfect" (Romans 12:2). Your life of prayer can grow as you follow a pattern, learn disciplines of prayer, and experience the results of your prayer.

A PATTERN OF PRAYER

The life of prayer is evident in the Psalms as the psalmists repeatedly cry out to God. We learn that conversation with God, lifting our soul to Him, is something we can do in every circumstance of life. As you read through the Psalms you will notice four main categories of prayer forming a pattern for you—the familiar acrostic ACTS:

> *Adoration*—"I love You, O LORD my strength" (Psalm 18:1).

> *Confession*—"Against You, You only, I have sinned" (Psalm 51:4).

> *Thanksgiving*—"I will give thanks to You, O Lord, among the peoples" (Psalm 57:9).

> *Supplication*—"Be gracious to me, O God, according to Your lovingkindness" (Psalm 51:1).

As a guideline, these four areas may be used many ways. Some days you may emphasize adoration and worship of God. Other days confession of sin will be the focus. Sometimes supplication will be the highlight as you lay burdens for your family and friends at the feet of the Lord. Familiarize yourself with these areas of prayer, using them to commune and interact with God, lifting your soul to Him. The best way to learn to pray is to ask the Lord to hear you and then pray.

Adoration

To adore God, you may begin with stillness, turning your thoughts to the knowledge that He is God. Think about what you have learned about God and His ways in your quiet time. Worship Him, thinking about every facet of His nature. God loves to be remembered by you and delights in hearing your expressions of love for Him (Deuteronomy 11:22; Psalm 31:23; Psalm 34:1). You might turn to the Psalms, using their words to magnify and exalt the Lord. Or you may choose to write a psalm in your journal, personalizing it as a way of talking with God. You may play a favorite praise tape to worship the Lord. Another way to adore God is to meditate on the names of God, praising God for who He is and what He does.

Confession

As you grow in the knowledge and grace of the Lord in your quiet time, He reveals attitudes and actions requiring inner transformation in your life. He discloses sin in your life with forgiveness, not condemnation (Romans 8:1). This forgiveness cost God the life of His beloved Son, Jesus Christ (John 3:16). Therefore, receive this forgiveness with a humble and grateful heart. "If we confess our sins, He is faithful and righteous to forgive us our sins and to cleanse us from all unrighteousness" (1 John 1:9). The word *confess* means "to agree with God or say the same thing as God does about your sin."[1] Come before God and ask Him to search your heart, reveal unpleasing areas of your life, and conform you to the image of Christ Jesus (Romans 8:29).

Thanksgiving

In thanksgiving, focus on God's blessings. One of the most repeated words throughout the Bible is *blessed,* meaning "to be fully satisfied."[2] Zodhiates observes, "The blessed person is one whom God makes fully satisfied, not because of favorable circumstances, but because He indwells the believer through Christ."[3] Our satisfaction comes from God, "who has blessed us with every spiritual blessing in the heavenly places in Christ" (Ephesians 1:3). God's blessings include our families, material goods, and even circumstances. Turn your thoughts to God's spiritual and material gifts in your life. Write a prayer of thanksgiving to the Lord. Paul encourages us to give thanks in everything (1 Thessalonians 5:18) and give thanks for all things "in the name of our Lord Jesus Christ to God, even the Father" (Ephesians 5:20). One writer has said that thanksgiving is "the fruit of a deliberate resolve to think about God, ourselves, and our privileges and responsibilities. By giving thanks we make manifest the fact that our lives are not controlled by the imperious concerns of this life. We give testimony to the fact that material things do not dictate the horizons of our soul."[4] My mother likes to write out five things each day for which she is thankful. This is such a great idea. When you do this, you will see gifts and blessings of God you may not have noticed before. A spirit of thanksgiving will grow in your heart. May we be like the healed leper who turned back and fell on his face at the feet of Jesus, giving thanks to Him for all He had done on his behalf (Luke 17:11-19).

Supplication

Supplication means "making your requests known to God." Bringing your requests to the throne of God is the special privilege of every child of God. Supplication is encouraged throughout Scripture (Philippians 4:6-7; John 15:7; Matthew 7:7-8; 1 John 5:14-15). Part of supplication is listening to God in His Word. In fact, you may choose a passage of Scripture and personalize the words to form a prayer to the Lord. Begin with the Psalms and then move to other passages of Scripture. When you pray the Word, you may be assured that you are praying according to God's will because Scripture is an expression of His desires. Often during prayer, God changes the desires of your heart, forming a new prayer. Sometimes God has said no to one prayer to say yes to His best, leading me to pray, "Lord, keep my dreams and desires within the boundaries of Your plans." We may boldly approach God, knowing that He will incline to us, hear our cries (Psalm 40:1), and act on our behalf (Isaiah 64:4).

WHAT TO PRAY FOR DAILY ACCORDING TO GOD'S WORD

- To be filled with the Holy Spirit (Ephesians 5:18)
- To walk in a manner worthy of the Lord (Colossians 1:10)

- To please God in all respects (Colossians 1:10)

- That the love of God would be shed abroad in your heart (Romans 5:5 KJV)

- That you might know God and Jesus Christ (Philippians 3:8)

- That God might search and know your heart (Psalm 139:23)

- To be conformed to the image of Christ (Romans 8:29)

- To clothe you with your spiritual armor (Ephesians 6:13-17)

- To send out workers for the harvest (Luke 10:2)

- That those in your life would be strengthened with power and know the love of Christ (Ephesians 3:14-20)

- For the salvation of those around you (John 1:12-13)

DISCIPLINES OF PRAYER

Prayer is something you learn. It does not just happen, but grows with time and intention. No wonder the disciples asked Jesus, "Lord, teach us to pray" (Luke 11:1). May that become the prayer for all who are on the journey to radical intimacy.

One day I read the following words in my quiet time: "And pray in the Spirit on all occasions with all kinds of prayers and requests. With this in mind, be alert and always keep on praying for all the saints" (Ephesians 6:18 NIV). Convicted about the priority of prayer, I set out on a quest to become more of a prayer warrior, ready at all times to pray in the heat of the battle. I prayed, *Lord, teach me to pray.* Over the years, God has used the following disciplines to revolutionize my life of prayer.

Write Out Prayer Requests

Organize prayer according to daily and weekly requests and then watch how God works in your life. Use notebook paper or the preprinted pages in the "Adore God in Prayer" section of your *Quiet Time Notebook* (see the example on page 159). Written requests remind you of others' needs, but you may not always pray through every written request each day. Dated requests help you see how God answers your prayers. When I was single, I prayed fervently for my future husband on a particular day and wrote my request in my notebook. Months later I became engaged. My future husband, David, informed me he had prayed for me on his birthday. Much to my amazement, I looked in my notebook and discovered we had prayed on the exact same date! Prayer becomes an exciting adventure when you watch God at work.

Use Scripture in Prayer

Scripture is the best resource for your prayers. Prayers in the Bible may guide your own prayers. For example, Paul prays for the Colossian church to be filled with the knowledge of God's will, that they may "walk in a manner worthy of the Lord, to please Him in all respects, bearing fruit in every good work and increasing in the knowledge of God" (Colossians 1:10). God's commands can stimulate you to make a specific request: "Beloved, let us love one another, for love is from God; and everyone who loves is born of God and knows God" (1 John 4:7). This particular command may lead you to ask God to demonstrate His love through you. It may also reveal a lack of love, leading you to confession. A verse in your quiet time may prompt you to pray, using the words as a guideline.

Prayer Resources

I have enjoyed using many resources in my own life of prayer. You might use 3 x 5 cards to carry specific requests with you throughout the day. Write verses on your prayer pages as support for your requests. Many Bible promise books list promises to claim as you pray. The Praying God's Will series compiled by Lee Roberts (published by Thomas Nelson Publishers) contains Scripture organized topically, enabling you to pray God's will for your life, husband, wife, daughter, son, or marriage. Another prayer resource is the *Quiet Time Notebook*, offering prayer pages for prayer requests (see Figure 8).

Adore God In Prayer

"Don't worry about anything;
instead, pray about everything." Phil. 4:6 NLT

Prayer For Bible Study

Date: 6-20-95   Topic: Rev. study
Scripture: Deuteronomy 31:8
Request: Father, prepare our hearts for our study this
    coming year. Transform our lives with your
    Word this year.
Answer:

Date: 8-30-95   Topic: my teaching
Scripture: James 1:5
Request: Lord, please give me wisdom as I study and
    prepare our discussions. Give me a listening
    ear, sensitive to your guidance.
Answer:

Date: 9-15-95   Topic: class
Scripture: Acts 17:11
Request: Lord, put it in the hearts of the students to
    study hard, seeking You with all their hearts
    and souls.
Answer: 9-30-95 Thank You Lord for these great students

Date: 10-1-95   Topic: prophecy
Scripture: John 16:13
Request: Give us understanding into the prophecy of
    Daniel, especially the 70 weeks.

Answer: 10-15-95 Thank you for showing us Daniel
    9:25-27

The Quiet Time Notebook © 1994, 2005 Catherine Martin

Figure 8. Prayer page from *The Quiet Time Notebook*.

Learn About Prayer

Growth in prayer is a discipline. Use your concordance and look up all the occurrences of *pray* and *prayer,* reflecting on what you learn. When you discover an example of prayer in the Bible, write your insights in your journal. In the *Quiet Time Notebook,* these pages may be moved to the "Adore God in Prayer" section for contemplation during your times of prayer. I also like to collect quotes and illustrations about prayer from books, radio messages, sermons, conferences, audios, videos, and DVDs. I read them again and again for encouragement to pray. Also, always include one book on prayer in your quiet time for occasional reading and reflection. See appendix 4 for some of the classic books on prayer.

Pray for God's World

The more time you spend in the Bible, the more you share the heart and burdens of God. Because God desires to reach peoples of all nations with the gospel, your prayers will embrace the world. *Operation World* by Patrick Johnstone contains statistics, missionary endeavors, and country descriptions for every nation of the world. Using this tool, you can pray for the entire world in a year. One evening I opened *Operation World,* turned to the country of Tanzania, and fervently prayed through all the requests. Though I was unfamiliar with this country, I felt burdened for it. The next morning the newspaper featured unrest in Tanzania! Only God can move your heart to pray for what He sees in the world.

Posture in Prayer

The posture of your heart in reverence to God is more important than your physical posture. However, bowing your knees before God or lying prostrate on the floor at times encourages humility. Sometimes you may pray out loud as a reminder of God's presence and fellowship. Respond spontaneously in prayer when you sense the need and desire to talk with God.

When There Are No Words

Sometimes it seems as though God does not hear your prayer and there is only silence from heaven. Some have called this experience "the dark night of the soul." All blessings seem to be withheld from you. The psalmist says, "He who dwells in the shelter of the Most High will abide in the shadow of the Almighty" (Psalm 91:1). Your darkness may be the shadow of the great presence of the Almighty. God has not withdrawn from you. He holds you in His hands and will not let go. He encourages you by saying, "Do not fear, for I am with you; do not anxiously look about you, for I am your God. I will strengthen you, surely I will help you, surely I will uphold you with My righteous right hand" (Isaiah 41:10). When you are in the darkness with no more words to say, still there remains a prayer. It is the prayer offered by Jesus and the Holy Spirit. "The Spirit also helps our weakness; for we do not know how to pray as we should, but the Spirit Himself intercedes for us with groanings too deep for words; and He who searches the hearts knows what the mind of the Spirit is, because He intercedes for the saints according to the will of God" (Romans 8:26-27). Jesus, who is at the right hand of God, also intercedes for us (Romans 8:34). Therefore, wait for the Lord and be of good courage. God has not abandoned you. His plans are greater than the boundaries of your present experience in prayer. Hannah did not receive her answer for many years. As she learned to wait on the Lord, God matured her to be the mother of Samuel, God's prophet for a whole generation of His chosen people. Hannah's disappointment, her dark night of the soul, became God's appointment at the proper time (1 Samuel 1–2). In the trials of life, draw near to the Lord and pray. Your prayer of faith pleases God. The psalmist says, "Dwell in the land and cultivate faithfulness. Delight yourself in the Lord; and He will give you the desires of your heart. Commit your way to the Lord, trust also in Him, and He will do it. He will bring forth your righteousness as the light and your judgment as the noonday. Rest in the Lord and wait patiently for Him" (Psalm 37:3-7).

THE RESULT OF PRAYER

Bill Hybels says "a prayer warrior is a person who is convinced that God is omnipotent—that God has power to do anything, to change anyone and to intervene in any circumstance. A person who truly believes this refuses to doubt God." I would add that a person who truly believes this *will pray*. Your prayers to God are influential in the lives of those around you. You have been chosen to participate with God in His plans. God will answer your prayers, and you will see the evidence all around you. He commands and calls us to a life of prayer. Praying to God is not the only thing you can do, but it is the greatest thing you can do. "The effective prayer of a righteous man can accomplish much" (James 5:16). God desires to hear your voice, have your fellowship, and expand your confidence and trust. "The people who know their God will display strength and take action" (Daniel 11:32). God will continually give you the ability to do things beyond the limits of your own abilities. Jesus said, "He who believes in Me, as the Scripture said, 'From his innermost being will flow rivers of living water'" (John 7:38). Launch out on the great promises of God, claiming them as your very own. Your experience with God will move from a journey to what Corrie Ten Boom calls the life of FAITH: a Fantastic Adventure In Trusting Him.

My Response

DATE:

KEY VERSE: "So let us come boldly to the throne of our gracious God. There we will receive his mercy, and we will find grace to help us when we need it" (Hebrews 4:16 NLT).

FOR FURTHER THOUGHT: How is your life of prayer? Do you pray? Do you pray for your friends and family? Do you pray for your own personal needs? What would you like to see happen in your life of prayer?

MY RESPONSE:

SECRET FOUR: YIELD YOURSELF TO GOD

Though He slay me, I will hope in Him.

JOB 13:15

～⌒∂⌒～

God's ways are higher than your ways (Isaiah 55:8-9). We need to yield to His ways in humility and submission. This is the practical application of our faith and the reason Yield Yourself to God is the critical component of the P.R.A.Y.E.R. Quiet Time Plan. Our natural tendency is toward arrogance, pride, and self-centeredness. Humility is "the recognition of personal insufficiency of one's self but the powerful sufficiency of God."[1] There are those defining moments in our lives when we choose to yield rather than resist God's best. Abraham's moment was the offering of Isaac in obedience to God's command. Moses yielded to God's direction to lead the people out of Egypt. Jesus demonstrated humility when He became obedient to death on the cross, thus accomplishing the will of God (Philippians 2:8-11).

God wants you to follow His lead even though it doesn't fit into your plans, your heartache is unimaginable, or you do not understand God's ways.

In every Christian's life, the very foundations are sometimes shaken and God's character seems to be called into question. God brings us to a point of decision, a surrender that says, *God, whatever happens, I am Yours. I yield myself to You.* This yielding is a radical obedience reflected in Job's cry: "Though He slay me, I will hope in Him" (Job 13:15). Hannah Whitall Smith, a Quaker in the 1800s, mired in a bitter, disappointing marriage, came to her own point of surrender one distraught night, writing about "the loneliness of a heart made for God, but which has not yet reached its full satisfaction in Him." She learned that no one but God can fully satisfy a heart.

Paul says in Romans 12:1-2 (NLT), "And so, dear Christian friends, I plead with you to give your bodies to God. Let them be a living and holy sacrifice—the kind he will accept. When you think of what he has done for you, is this too much to ask? Don't copy the behavior and customs of this world, but let God transform you into a new person by changing the way you think. Then you will know what God wants you to do, and you will know how good and pleasing and perfect his will really is." God is speaking of full surrender, saying "Yes, Lord," to whatever He asks, even if it is completely different from what we had in mind. *Consecration* means offering ourselves to God with no strings attached. God is free to accomplish His will in our lives.

THE MOTIVATION FOR SURRENDER

The mercies of God are our motivation for surrender. They are the doctrine leading to duty, and they inspire belief, which leads to behavior. The New American Standard Bible translates "what he has done for you" (Romans 12:1-2 NLT) into "by the mercies of God," emphasizing that the Lord motivates with love rather than power. He wants us to choose Him and love Him out of gratitude for who He is and what He has done through the death of Jesus on the cross.

- Jesus Christ accomplished *redemption* for us. We are "justified as a gift by His grace through the redemption which is in Christ Jesus" (Romans 3:24). *Redemption* means "to purchase in the marketplace." We are set free by the death of Christ.

- Jesus Christ accomplished *propitiation* for us. Romans 3:25 describes Christ as one "whom God displayed publicly as a propitiation in His blood through faith." Christ's death fully satisfied all the righteous demands of God.

- Jesus Christ has accomplished *atonement* for us. "In Him we have redemption through His blood, the forgiveness of our trespasses" (Ephesians 1:7). Hebrews 9:22 (NIV) tells us that "without the shedding of blood there is no forgiveness."

- Jesus accomplished *justification* for us. "Through one act of righteousness there resulted justification of life to all men" (Romans 5:18). *Justification* means to "declare righteous."

- Jesus accomplished *reconciliation* for us. "For if while we were enemies we were reconciled to God through the death of His Son, much more, having been reconciled, we shall be saved by His life" (Romans 5:10). God has changed toward us, and we may now be friends with Him through Jesus Christ.

- Jesus accomplished *adoption* for us. Romans 8:15 says, "For you have not received a spirit of slavery leading to fear again, but you have received a spirit of adoption as sons by which we cry out, 'Abba! Father!'" Our adoption means we may have the childlike trust to call God our Father.

- Jesus Christ accomplished *sanctification* for us. "But now having been freed from sin and enslaved to God, you derive your benefit, resulting in sanctification" (Romans 6:22). *Sanctification* in the Greek language is *hagiasmos* and means "holiness," referring to the process of being set apart for God's service and reflecting His character.[2]

- Jesus has accomplished *glorification* for us. "Whom He predestined, He also called; and these whom He called, He also justified; and these whom He justified, He also glorified" (Romans 8:30). Our glorification means God is going to wipe every tear from our eyes and invite us to enter the great city of God.

In light of these mercies, God desires our wholehearted devotion. He wants us to come to Him and say, *Here I am, Lord. Use me as you will. Wherever, whatever, it's okay. I will trust you no matter what happens. I am Yours; I surrender all to You.* For some, surrender may seem easy. What if you, like Hannah Whitall Smith, are married to someone who is antagonistic to the Lord and to you? What if you are in a job seemingly void of meaning? What if you have a physical disability and can no longer walk? What if you feel insignificant in the great scheme of life? These things were not what we dreamed of when we gave our life to God. And yet, these are the trials that bring us to the kind of wholehearted "presenting of our bodies to God" that Paul describes in Romans 12:1-2. The very circumstance you resist can produce the surrender you need.

Hannah Whitall Smith describes her own surrender in her trials:

> It was at a time in my religious life when I was passing through a great deal of questioning and perplexity, and I felt that no Christian had ever had such peculiar difficulties as mine before. There happened to be staying near me just then for a few weeks a lady who was considered to be a deeply spiritual Christian, and to whom I had been advised to apply for spiritual help. I summoned up my courage, therefore, one afternoon and went to see her, pouring out my troubles; I expected of course that she would take a deep interest in me, and would be at great pains to do all she could to help me. She listened patiently enough, and did not interrupt me; but when I had finished my story, and had paused, expecting sympathy and consideration, she simply said, "Yes all you say may be very true, but then, in spite of it all, there is God." I waited a few minutes for something more, but nothing came, and my friend and teacher had the air of having said all that was necessary. But, I continued, surely you did not understand how very serious and perplexing my difficulties are. Oh Yes I did, replied my friend, but then, as I tell you, there is God. And I could not induce her to make

any other answer. It seemed to me most disappointing and unsatisfactory. I felt that my peculiar and really harrowing experiences could not be met by anything so simple as merely the statement, Yes but there is God. I knew God was there, of course, but I felt I needed something more than just God; and I came to the conclusion that my friend, for all her great reputation as a spiritual teacher, was at any rate not able to grapple with a peculiar case such as mine. However, my need was so great that I did not give up with my first trial, but went to her again and again, always with the hope that she would sometime begin to understand the importance of my difficulties and would give me adequate help. It was of no avail. I was never able to draw forth any other answer… and at last because she said it so often and seemed so sure, I began to dimly wonder whether after all God might not be enough even for my need, overwhelming and peculiar as I felt it to be. From wondering I came gradually to believing that, being my Creator and Redeemer, He must be enough; and at last a conviction burst upon me that He really was enough, and my eyes were opened to the fact of the absolute and utter all-sufficiency of God. My troubles disappeared like magic, and I did nothing but wonder how I could ever have been such an idiot as to be troubled by them, when all the while there was God, the Almighty and all-seeing God, the God who had created me, and was therefore on my side and eager to care for me and help me. I had found out that God was enough and my soul was at rest.

My Response

DATE:

KEY VERSE: "And so, dear Christian friends, I plead with you to give your bodies to God. Let them be a living and holy sacrifice—the kind he will accept. When you think of what he has done for you, is this too much to ask? Don't copy the behavior and customs of this world, but let God transform you into a new person by changing the way you think. Then you will know what God wants you to do, and you will know how good and pleasing and perfect his will really is" (Romans 12:1-2 NLT).

FOR FURTHER THOUGHT: What is your favorite mercy of God that is the proof of God's amazing love as described in this day? In view of God's mercies, have you surrendered all to the Lord?

MY RESPONSE:

Day Twenty-One

A JOURNEY OF SURRENDER

The mind of man plans his way,
but the LORD directs his steps.

PROVERBS 16:9

Surrender is a necessary grace, but it is not a natural one. Proverbs 16:9 says, "The mind of man plans his way, but the LORD directs his steps." To surrender, we need the grace of God and the power of His Spirit. Peter encourages believers to "humble yourselves under the mighty hand of God, that He may exalt you at the proper time, casting all your anxiety on Him, because He cares for you" (1 Peter 5:6-7).

When I joined the staff of Campus Crusade, I longed for placement on a college campus where I could begin my dream to disciple women. Much to my surprise and dismay, I was placed in a position as a secretary rather than as a campus minister. All I saw was the moment—the now—and the position—secretary. It never occurred to me at the time that God might be placing me in the company of one of the top Christian speakers in the world, Josh McDowell, so I could learn about all facets of ministry. I could have said no to God, but I chose to yield to Him.

Yes, Lord. Whatever happens, I am Yours. I yield myself to You.

Years later, still yearning to disciple women, I was blessed to become involved with Bible Study Fellowship and Precept Ministries International. After I got married, my husband encouraged me to go to seminary, expanding the vision and dreams in my heart. Maybe I would teach at a Christian university or seminary someday. Juggling a full-time job with intense study, I wondered whether I could complete such an arduous task. Was I willing to pay the price in time and energy to finish the course?

Yes, Lord. Whatever happens, I am Yours. I yield myself to You.

I've read that "sometimes God will shatter your dreams to broaden your vision." Following seminary, I had become content living in San Diego. New opportunities had opened up with the birth of Quiet Time Ministries. Then one day I received the news that we were leaving San Diego to move to Palm Springs. I was devastated because I thought the move represented the end of my dreams. I had no friends there, not even a church family; I thought my life and ministry had ended. Looking for comfort, I studied Psalm 84, verse 5 literally leaping off the page at me: "Blessed are those whose strength is in you [the Lord], who have set their hearts on pilgrimage" (Psalm 84:5 NIV). I prayed, "Lord, now I see You are showing me that life is a *pilgrimage of the heart.*" I fell before the Lord in surrender to Him.

With that surrender, God's plan for my life soon opened before me. Within months, I was asked to be Director of Women's Ministries at a large church in the Palm Springs area. Soon thereafter, I joined the adjunct faculty of Biola University to teach Bible courses, Christian worldview and theology, and the Christian life. Finally, Quiet Time Ministries grew to become worldwide in scope with the publishing of quiet times by NavPress.

Yes, Lord. Whatever happens, I am Yours. I yield myself to You.

The Means to Surrender

J. Sidlow Baxter says, "How wonderful beyond words is that tragic yet magnetic Cross! In it the deadliest sin of fallen man becomes the purest triumph of divine love." The mercies of God (Romans 12:1) described throughout Romans influence us, leading to surrender and yield to God.

- The mercies of God *humble* us. Martin Luther emphasized that God creates out of nothing. Therefore, until a man is nothing, God can make nothing out of him. So often, we wrestle with how God orchestrates the events in our life. We think, *If only God would do this my way, everything would work out.* When things don't go your way, "humble [yourself] under the mighty hand of God, that He may exalt you at the proper time" (1 Peter 5:6). Looking at the sovereign plan of God in Christ's death on the cross will help you bend the knee in submission and worship.

- The mercies of God *uplift* us. When you survey these great truths of God, you realize the enormity of God's plan, and you rise above your circumstances.

- The mercies of God *melt our hearts.* Seeing the great love of God demonstrated in Jesus Christ softens your heart.

- The mercies of God *break* us. Brokenness brings you to a place where you have no further plans of your own. The broken heart wants only what God wants. The psalmist tells us that "the LORD is near to the brokenhearted and saves those who are crushed in spirit" (Psalm 34:18). In your deepest suffering, God Himself will carry you to the place of surrender.

- The mercies of God *liberate* us. We see that God is God, sovereign and perfectly in control. He is love and loves us. These truths give us the ability to yield because if God knows everything and God is good, we can trust His heart.

- The mercies of God *encourage* us. Even if life does not seem to be going your way, you no longer interpret God by your circumstances but by His Word. Then you are encouraged regardless of what happens in your life.

So often we want our own plans, not realizing that God has something else in mind. Yield yourself to God and give Him free reign in your life. Peter shares this promise from God: "After you have suffered for a little while, the God of all grace, who called you to His eternal glory in Christ, will Himself perfect, confirm, strengthen and establish you" (1 Peter 5:10). Some people have said that God always gives the best to those who leave the choice to Him. Oswald Chambers calls surrender "giving up my right to myself."[1] Hold nothing back—no earthly life, no material gain, no pride-filled position—but simply say…

Yes, Lord. Whatever happens, I am Yours. I yield myself to You.

Your quiet time is the ideal place to express your surrender to God. Use David's example of surrender and commitment in his psalms. Open up your heart. Pray it. Sing it. Then write your prayers of commitment and affirmation to the Lord in your *Quiet Time Notebook* (see Figure 9 on the next page).

A Christian woman asked her minister, "What is your idea of surrender to God?" Holding out a blank sheet of paper, the pastor replied, "It is to sign your name at the bottom of this blank sheet and to let God fill it in as He will."

Date: *Jan 21, 2005*

As you close your quiet time, spend a few moments reflecting on applying the truth of the Word of God in your own relationship with the Lord.

Yield Yourself To God
: Place any unfulfilled dreams and desires in the hands of the Lord. If you sense a particular need today to humble yourself under God's mighty hand, that He may lift you up in due time (1 Peter 5:6), write a brief prayer expressing all that is on your heart.

Lord, keep my dreams and desires within the boundaries of Your plans. Enable me to be faithful and reflect You to those around me.

Enjoy His Presence
: Place today's responsibilities, activities, and appointments in the hands of the Lord.

Special Requests For Today:

Boldness from the Holy Spirit as I share my testimony

One Significant Insight To Think About Today:

God wants me to dwell on eternal truths found in His Word.

Rest In His Love
: As you close your time with the Lord, place any anxious thoughts, conflicts, or difficult circumstances in the hands of the Lord. Record a promise or verse from God's Word related to your particular need.

Philippians 4:13 I can do everything through Him who gives me strength

"...let us run with perseverance the race marked out for us. Let us fix our eyes on Jesus, the author and perfecter of our faith..." Hebrews 12:1-2 NIV

Figure 9. "Yield, Enjoy, Rest" page from *The Quiet Time Notebook*.

This page offers practical application for your quiet time.

My Response

DATE:

KEY VERSE: "Therefore humble yourselves under the mighty hand of God, that He may exalt you at the proper time, casting all your anxiety on Him, because He cares for you" (1 Peter 5:6-7).

FOR FURTHER THOUGHT: How has God worked in your life over the last few years? What things have you had to lay at His feet in order to follow Him? Are there dreams and desires that you need to give to the Lord now in order to continue on in this great adventure of knowing God? Are you willing to sign your name at the bottom of a blank page and let God fill it in as He will? You can trust Him to have the very best plan for your life. Remember, God says: "'For I know the plans that I have for you,' declares the LORD, 'plans for welfare and not for calamity to give you a future and a hope'" (Jeremiah 29:11). Write your thoughts in the space provided.

MY RESPONSE:

Day Twenty-Two

SECRET FIVE:
ENJOY HIS PRESENCE

Never will I leave you;
never will I forsake you.

HEBREWS 13:5 NIV

God's presence means you are never alone. The Bible speaks of an unceasing life with God (1 Thessalonians 5:17). He is your constant companion, encouraging you in every circumstance of life (2 Timothy 4:17). Jesus promises to never leave you or forsake you and to give you His joy (Hebrews 13:5, John 15:11). Because of this promise, at any time during the day, you may Enjoy His Presence.

Nicholas Herman of Lorraine, who lived in the 1600s, was captured in the Thirty Year War at the age of 18, charged with espionage, and threatened with hanging. He proclaimed his innocence and was released, his military service ending when he was wounded. His war experience led him to give his life to Christ. At a Carmelite monastery, he became a monk and was given the name Brother Lawrence. He looked upon his job in the kitchen with disdain until one day he made a conscious decision to live in the presence of God moment by moment, walking and talking with Him throughout the day. He describes the result of that decision: "I suddenly found myself changed and my soul, which up till then was always disturbed, experienced a profound interior peace." *The Practice of the Presence of God*, a collection of his letters and reminiscences, was published at the end of the seventeenth century. In it he says, "The time of business does not with me differ from the time of prayer, and in the noise and clatter of my kitchen…I possess God in as great tranquility as if I were upon my knees at the blessed sacrament."

In his Ninth Letter, he encourages others to surrender prayers, thoughts, and actions to God throughout the day:

> We cannot escape the dangers which abound in life, without the actual and continual help of God; let us then pray to Him for it continually. How can we pray to Him without being with Him? How can we be with Him but in thinking of Him often? And how can we often think of Him, but by a holy habit which we should form of it? You will tell me that I am always saying the same thing: it is true, for this is the best and easiest method I know; and as I use no other, I advise all the world to it. We must know before we can love. In order to know God, we must often think of Him; and when we come to love Him, we shall then also think of Him often, for our heart will be with our treasure.

As you leave your quiet time, the Lord goes with you. Place your activities, responsibilities, and appointments in the hands of the Lord. Include Him in every circumstance; remember and embrace Him in everything you do. Frank Laubach expresses this desire to enjoy His presence:

> God, I want to give You every minute of this year. I shall try to keep You in mind every moment of my waking hours. I shall try to let my hand write what You direct. I shall try to let You be the speaker and direct every word. I shall try to let You direct my acts. I shall try to learn Your language as it was taught by Jesus and all others through whom You

speak—in beauty and singing birds and cool breezes, in radiant Christlike faces, in sacrifices and tears. It will cost not only much, but everything that conflicts with this resolve."[1]

BREAKFAST WITH THE LORD

About once a week, I gather my quiet time materials and seek out a favorite restaurant for breakfast with the Lord. After ordering a hot cup of coffee and a hearty breakfast, I settle into the Word and write in my journal, continually talking with God about what I am learning and how much I enjoy being with Him. I usually close my time with meditation in a favorite devotional reading. These special moments have inspired books such as *Revive My Heart!*, messages such as "What's It All About?", and ideas for ministry such as *The Quiet Time Notebook*.

DAY WITH THE LORD

Occasionally, I schedule a personal, spiritual retreat as a day with the Lord. Ladislaus Boros has said, "Everything true and great grows in silence." Can you imagine a paragraph with no periods or spaces? How could you understand the meaning? Your heart and soul need quiet places and times with God in order for your relationship with God to grow and flourish.

During your personal retreat you will use the spiritual disciplines of solitude and silence, journaling, devotional reading, and meditating on God's Word as ways to draw near to Him. Emilie Griffin says this: "Spiritual disciplines are ways to truth, stepping stones from our furious activity into God's calm and peace. When we have crossed over on the stepping stones, we escape into the life of grace."[2] The rapid pace of the current age drains the heart, so we are driven to search out the deeper graces for the soul. A day with the Lord is a vacation for the soul.

- Schedule a time for your retreat and write it in your datebook. It may be only a few hours one afternoon in the park or two days away at a lodge in the mountains.

- Search out a place conducive to your retreat with God—safe, quiet, and pleasing to the senses. Many of these places are listed in books such as *Sanctuaries* by Marcia and Jack Kelly and *A Place for God* by Timothy Jones.

- Formulate a plan by gathering your vital quiet time materials. These may include a Bible, *The Quiet Time Notebook* or a journal, laptop computer, devotional reading, audio cassette or CD player, worship music, teaching tapes or CDs, snacks, beverages, coffeemaker/coffee/travel mug, warm clothing if you're in the mountains, backpack for materials if you're going to go hiking, Quiet Time Ministries materials, and even a camera for photography. Nature photography can calm your spirit and give you remembrances of your time with the Lord. An artist might take a sketch pad or watercolors. Bring those things that nurture the creative part of your personality.

A Sample Schedule for a Day with the Lord

- Prepare Your Heart from 9:00 to 10:00 AM by reading from a book such as *Knowing God* by J.I. Packer or *The Pursuit of God* by A.W. Tozer.

- Read and Study God's Word from 10:00 to 11:00 AM. Try reading Hebrews 11 and writing out everything you learn about faith.

- Adore God in Prayer from 11:00 AM to noon by writing a prayer to the Lord, listening to worship music, and meditating on words from a hymnbook.

- With your Bible, a devotional book, and your journal, enjoy a leisurely lunch with the Lord from noon to 2:00.

- Yield Yourself to God from 2:00 to 3:00 PM by reading from a devotional or enjoying a quiet time from one of the books of quiet times: *Pilgrimage of the Heart, Revive My Heart!, A Heart That Dances, A Heart on Fire,* or *A Heart to See Forever.*

- Enjoy His Presence from 3:00 to 4:00 PM by going for a nature walk with God and taking pictures.

- Rest in His Love from 4:00 to 4:30 by meditating on all you have learned and writing in your journal.

My Response

DATE:

KEY VERSE: "The LORD is the one who goes ahead of you; He will be with you. He will not fail you or forsake you. Do not fear or be dismayed" (Deuteronomy 31:8).

FOR FURTHER THOUGHT: How can you enjoy the presence of the Lord today? Will you set aside time and do something special, such as going for a walk with the Lord or sitting and listening to praise music? You might even choose to go on a personal retreat with the Lord, such as going to breakfast or going to a park to commune with Him.

MY RESPONSE:

Day Twenty-Three

SECRET SIX:
REST IN HIS LOVE

*Come to Me, all who are weary and
heavy-laden, and I will give you rest.*

MATTHEW 11:28

Radical intimacy is the one thing no one can touch. Radical intimacy brings a surprise experience of God's love, independent of all feelings and circumstances. And in that love you will find rest for your soul, even in the most difficult of times. As you close your quiet time with the Lord, you will Rest in His Love, the final element in the P.R.A.Y.E.R. Quiet Time Plan. Jesus encouraged His disciples with these words: "Are you tired? Worn out? Burned out on religion? Come to me. Get away with me and you'll recover your life. I'll show you how to take a real rest. Walk with me and work with me—watch how I do it. Learn the unforced rhythms of grace. I won't lay anything heavy or ill-fitting on you. Keep company with me and you'll learn to live freely and lightly" (Matthew 11:28-30 MSG).

In another translation of Matthew 11:28-30, Jesus says, "Come to Me, all who are weary and heavy-laden, and I will give you rest. Take My yoke upon you and learn from Me, for I am gentle and humble in heart, and you will find rest for your souls. For My yoke is easy and My burden is light." When Jesus says, "Come to Me," He is inviting those who are weary and lonely to share His life. This is what radical intimacy with the Lord is all about. Jesus is the answer for every problem that comes your way.

- Jesus invites you to "come to Me." The result of coming to Jesus is rest, refreshment, and relief. "Times of refreshing may come from the presence of the Lord" (Acts 3:19) even in the midst of crushing burdens.

- Jesus invites you to "take My yoke upon you." A yoke is a heavy piece of wood that hitched a team of animals together to work in unison and pull heavy loads. We are yoked to Jesus by His love, mercy, grace, and forgiveness. Jesus binds you to Himself that you might live life with Him in an eternal relationship, never to be alone again. The result is relief from the heaviness of burdens. He says, "My yoke is easy and My burden is light." You will experience the easy yoke and the light burden of His character and ways; a true rest in His love.

- Jesus invites you to "learn from Me." Jesus desires your commitment to learn from Him; this is His invitation to discipleship. In the Greek, the word *learn* means to "know something and bring it into your own experience." You actually bring Jesus—His character, Person, and words— into every part of your life. As His disciple, you sit at His feet and listen to His words.

- Jesus invites you to know His heart. Jesus reveals He is "gentle and humble in heart." He is meek and mild and utterly approachable. His humility compelled Him to leave the palace of heaven, come to earth, become a servant, take on human flesh, and die on a cross so our sins might be forgiven (Philippians 2).

- Jesus invites you to "find rest for your soul." The only way to find that rest is to come to Jesus, take His yoke upon you, and learn from Him.

A man was deer hunting in the wilds of Oregon. Cradling his rifle in the crook of his arm, he followed an old logging road nearly overgrown by the encroaching forest. All of a sudden, he heard a noise in the brush nearby. Before he even had a chance to lift his rifle, a small blur of brown and white rushed up the road straight for him. It all happened so fast, he didn't even have time to think. He looked down and saw a little brown cottontail rabbit—its little heart racing like the wind—crowded up against his legs between his boots. The little thing was trembling all over, but it just sat there and didn't budge. This was especially strange because wild rabbits are afraid of people and usually will not come close enough to sit at your feet. Then, down the road, a weasel burst out of the brush. When it saw the man and its intended prey sitting at the man's feet, the predator froze in its tracks, its mouth panting, its eyes glowing red. It was then that the hunter understood he had stepped into a life-and-death drama in the forest. The cottontail, exhausted by the chase, was only moments from death. The man was its last hope of refuge. Forgetting its natural fear and caution, the little animal instinctively crowded up against him for protection, away from the sharp teeth of its relentless enemy. The man lifted his powerful rifle and shot into the ground just underneath the weasel. The animal leaped straight into the air and then rocketed back into the forest as fast as its legs could move. For a while, the little rabbit didn't stir. It just sat there, huddled at the man's feet in the gathering twilight while he spoke gently to it. "Where did it go, little one? I don't think he'll be bothering you for a little while. Looks like you're off the hook tonight." Soon the rabbit hopped away from its protector into the forest.

Where do you run when the burden of sin is weighing you down? What do you do when you are so troubled you cannot speak? Where is your refuge when the circumstances are overwhelming? Turn to the only One who stands with arms open wide, waiting for you to come, that He might give you rest for your soul. Bring Him every care, thought, and burden of your heart. Then rest in His love.

O lover to the uttermost,
May I read the meltings of thy heart to me
In the manger of thy birth,
In the garden of thy agony,
In the cross of thy suffering,
In the tomb of thy resurrection
In the heaven of thy intercession.
Bold in this thought I defy my adversary,
Tread down his temptations,
Resist his schemings,
Renounce the world,
Am valiant for truth.
Deepen in me a sense of my holy relationship to thee,
As spiritual bridegroom,
As Jehovah's fellow,
As sinners' friend.
I think of thy glory and my vileness,
Thy majesty and my meanness,
Thy beauty and my deformity,
Thy purity and my filth,
Thy righteousness and my iniquity.
Thou hast loved me everlastingly, unchangeably,
May I love thee as I am loved;
Thou hast given thyself for me,
May I give myself to thee;
Thou hast died for me,
May I live to thee.
In every moment of my time,
In every movement of my mind,
In every pulse of my heart,
May I never dally with the world and its allurements,
But walk by thy side,
Listen to thy voice,
Be clothed with thy graces,
And adorned with thy righteousness.
In Jesus' name. Amen.[1]

The Valley of Vision

My Response

DATE:

KEY VERSE: "Come to Me, all who are weary and heavy-laden, and I will give you rest. Take My yoke upon you and learn from Me, for I am gentle and humble in heart, and you will find rest for your souls. For My yoke is easy and My burden is light" (Matthew 11:28-30).

FOR FURTHER THOUGHT: Describe your life right now. Have you scheduled punctuation marks in your life so that you can go to the Lord Jesus and find rest? What does it mean to rest in the Lord? What will it mean to you to find rest in the Lord? In what ways do you need His rest today?

MY RESPONSE:

Day Twenty-Four

QUIET TIME—
WEEK FOUR:
REACH THE SUMMITS

*Then Hezekiah took the letter from the
hands of the messengers and read it, and
he went up to the house of the LORD,
and spread it out before the LORD.*

2 KINGS 19:14

PREPARE YOUR HEART

Most people have heard about the influence of Evan Roberts in the Welsh Revival of 1904–1905. During that time, God also raised up another man of influence, Rees Howells, a simple coal miner whose heart was captured for Jesus Christ. Rees Howells was burdened to pray for all the new converts from the Welsh Revival to become committed disciples of Christ. He led the crusade for prayer everywhere he went. Following the main thrust of the Welsh Revival, he found a village that had not yet experienced revival. The Lord challenged him to personally pray for the people of this village. Soon revival swept through, and many were saved.

Howells founded a Bible college during World War II and led his students to become prayer warriors while men battled on the front lines. Howells and his wife later became missionaries in South Africa. As they visited mission stations throughout South Africa, revival broke out. God's provision of Rees Howells, a prayer warrior behind the scenes of the Welsh Revival, was God's magnificent design. Every great revival has come from a great outpouring of prayer. If revival is to come again, men and women must go to God in wholehearted prayer. The powerful statement in 2 Chronicles 16:9 is something to think about: "For the eyes of the LORD move to and fro throughout the earth that He may strongly support those whose heart is completely His." Take some time now to think about your own life of prayer. Will you pray the prayer of the disciples today: *Lord, teach me to pray?*

READ AND STUDY GOD'S WORD

1. Those who would desire a radical intimacy with the Lord will learn how to pray. One who knew the life of prayer was King Hezekiah. Read 2 Kings 18:1-6 and record everything you learn about Hezekiah.

2. During his reign as king of God's people, Hezekiah was faced with a difficult situation. Sennacherib, the king of

Assyria, threatened both Hezekiah and his people. He sent a strong letter to Hezekiah, indicating he would destroy both Hezekiah and his people and that Hezekiah's God would not save him. Read 2 Kings 19:14-37 and describe how Hezekiah handled the difficulty that came his way.

3. What did God do as a result?

4. Read the following verses and record everything you learn about prayer:

   Luke 5:15-16

   Philippians 4:6-7

1 Thessalonians 5:17

James 5:16

5. Summarize in two or three sentences what you have learned about prayer.

ADORE GOD IN PRAYER

Use the words of the Lord's Prayer from Matthew 6:9-13 for your prayer to the Lord today:

> Our Father, who is in heaven,
> Hallowed be Your name.
> Your kingdom come.
> Your will be done,
> On earth as it is in heaven.
> Give us this day our daily bread.
> And forgive us our debts, as we also have forgiven our debtors.
> And do not lead us into temptation, but deliver us from evil. [For Yours is the kingdom and the power and the glory forever. Amen.]

YIELD YOURSELF TO GOD

Prayer is the forerunner of mercy. Turn to sacred history, and you will find that scarcely ever did a great mercy come to this world unheralded by supplication. You have found this true in your own personal experience. God has given you many an unsolicited favour, but still great prayer has always been the prelude of great mercy with you. When you first found peace through the blood of the cross, you had been praying much, and earnestly interceding with God that he would remove your doubts, and deliver you from your distresses. Your assurance was the result of prayer. When at any time you have had high and rapturous joys, you have been obliged to look upon them as answers to your prayers. When you have had great deliverances out of sore troubles, and mighty helps in great dangers, you have been able to say, "I sought the Lord, and he heard me, and delivered me from all my fears." *Prayer* is always the preface to blessing. It goes before the blessing *as the blessing's shadow.* When the sunlight of God's mercies rises upon our necessities, it casts the shadow of prayer far down upon the plain. Or, to use another illustration, when God piles up a hill of mercies, he himself shines behind them, and he casts on our spirits the shadow of prayer, so that we may rest certain, if we are much in prayer, our pleadings are the shadows of mercy. Prayer is thus connected with the blessing *to show us the value of it.* If we had the blessings without asking for them, we should think them common things; but prayer makes our mercies more precious than diamonds. The things we ask for are precious, but we do not realize their preciousness until we have sought for them earnestly.

Prayer makes the darken'd cloud withdraw;
Prayer climbs the ladder Jacob saw;
Gives exercise to faith and love;
Brings every blessing from above.[1]

Charles Haddon Spurgeon
Morning and Evening

ENJOY HIS PRESENCE

How is your life of prayer these days? Oswald Chambers says that prayer is not preparation for the greater work, prayer is the greater work. Do you realize the amazing influence you can have for the kingdom of God when you drop all other things, draw near to the Lord, and pray? Write a prayer to the Lord today, expressing all that is on your heart.

REST IN HIS LOVE

"Be anxious for nothing, but in everything by prayer and supplication with thanksgiving let your requests be made known to God. And the peace of God, which surpasses all comprehension, will guard your hearts and your minds in Christ Jesus" (Philippians 4:6-7).

Week Five

ENJOY
THE VIEW

Days 25-30

Day Twenty-Five

PUTTING IT
ALL TOGETHER

Tune your ears to the world of Wisdom;
set your heart on a life of Understanding.

PROVERBS 2:2 MSG

ariety makes your quiet time a great adventure. The writer of Proverbs encourages you to "tune your ears to the world of Wisdom; set your heart on a life of Understanding. That's right—if you make Insight your priority, and won't take no for an answer, searching for it like a prospector panning for gold, like an adventurer on a treasure hunt, believe me, before you know it Fear-of-GOD will be yours; you'll have come upon the Knowledge of God" (Proverbs 2:2 MSG). Everything you have learned about quiet time gives you confidence to embark on the ultimate treasure hunt; the great adventure of knowing God.

In the musical *The Sound of Music,* Maria, as governess, teaches

Captain Von Trapp's seven children to sing using the octave scale of do, re, mi, fa, so, la, ti, do. Maria tells them that they can sing almost anything with those simple notes. Then she challenges them to put it all together. So it is with quiet time. Once you have learned the disciplines of devotion through the P.R.A.Y.E.R. Quiet Time Plan, you can combine those disciplines into a great adventure—your own personalized quiet time. Be creative! Expand one section and contract another; add in disciplines and delete others. Think of your quiet time as an accordion that can be expanded or contracted according to your time, desire, and the leading of the Holy Spirit. To help you begin, you might want to pray through the worksheet "Getting Started in Your Quiet Time" found in appendix 5 and plan your quiet time. If you would like quiet times already prepared for you, try the Quiet Times for the Heart series: *Pilgrimage of the Heart, Revive My Heart!,* and *A Heart That Dances* (published by NavPress), and *A Heart on Fire* and *A Heart to See Forever* (published by Quiet Time Ministries Press). These quiet times include all the devotional disciplines of the P.R.A.Y.E.R. Quiet Time Plan and are filled with devotional reading, hymns, biographies, devotional Bible study, prayer, and application to give you a daily, dynamic, interactive experience with the Lord.

A SIMPLE APPROACH

- *Prepare Your Heart.* Start with a psalm or the day's devotional reading in *My Utmost for His Highest* by Oswald Chambers, and write your insights in a journal.

- *Read and Study God's Word.* Read a passage of Scripture from a devotional Bible and cross-reference your favorite verse. Write one significant observation in your journal or your notebook.

- *Adore God in Prayer.* Talk with God about what you have read, the needs in your life, and anything else that is on your heart. Write your prayer requests on prayer pages in your notebook or write a prayer to the Lord in your journal.

- *Yield Yourself to God.* Write a prayer of commitment or surrender to the Lord. Meditate on what God has shown you in your quiet time and how you may apply it to your life.

- *Enjoy His Presence.* Plan how you can seek the presence of the Lord throughout the day. Talk with the Lord, commune with Him, and turn your entire attention to Him.

- *Rest in His Love.* Memorize a promise from God's Word that brings you comfort in your present circumstances.

HELPFUL HINTS

Focus on one detail. Be specific, not general. Sometimes, the Lord will slow you down to focus on only one word, idea, or phrase in His Word or in a devotional reading. Write about it, pray about it, yield to it, thank the Lord for it—and then take comfort in those words for the rest of the day. I have spent many quiet times simply contemplating the word "abide" from John 15. I have meditated on "God is my refuge" from Psalm 46. I have experienced supreme delight in some of my favorite quiet times by focusing on one song's chorus while listening to a wonderful worship CD.

Focus on one resource. When I lose my quiet time, I return to a classic book such as *Knowing God* by J.I. Packer or *The Pursuit of God* by A.W. Tozer. I can remember a quiet time when I sat down with the Lord, opened *Knowing God,* and spent more than an hour reading the chapter "These Inward Trials." I chose this chapter because it applied specifically to my current trial, and I wrote the most important quotes in my journal, adding my own insights. I read the important Bible verses Packer mentioned, and I meditated on those verses. Finally, I closed my quiet time by writing a prayer to the Lord in my quiet time notebook. In the same manner, *The Pursuit of God* produced a life-changing summer for me early in my relationship with God. I began my quiet time each day reading a portion of Tozer's book, turning to all the Scripture passages he used in the chapters, writing my insights in my notebook, and talking with God about all I had learned.

Focus on the Lord's leading. Be sensitive to the Lord's leading as you interact with Him in all the disciplines of devotion. If you read something that seems to touch your heart, stop and meditate on that one idea. Explore it, study it, write about it, and read commentaries on it. Who knows? Maybe that verse will become your life verse. Quiet time is ultimately a gift from the Lord. You have been faithful to have an arsenal of resources and disciplines to choose from, but the Lord is the One who will guide you and put it all together each day.

Focus on the goal. As you draw near to God each day, always keep your quiet time goal in mind: to know Him and to be radically intimate with Him. Think about those significant invitations to intimacy in the Bible: "Be still, and know that I am God" (Psalm 46:10 NKJV), "delight yourself in the LORD" (Psalm 37:4), "taste and see that the LORD is good" (Psalm 34:8), "draw near to God and He will draw near to you" (James 4:8). These words will help you see that your quiet time is not an academic exercise but a real experience with the living God. The result: radical intimacy.

There are a thousand and more ways to put it all together using the *P.R.A.Y.E.R.* Quiet Time Plan. The important thing is the great result: radical intimacy. Your intentional devotion as you experiment with the disciplines will take you to a deep level with the Lord, and you will see things you've never seen before, know what you've never known before, and become the man or woman God wants you to be. You will experience that great adventure of knowing the God of the universe, your Creator and Lord.

My Response

DATE:

KEY VERSE: "Taste and see that the LORD is good; how blessed is the man who takes refuge in Him!" (Psalm 34:8).

FOR FURTHER THOUGHT: Describe in your own words what quiet time is all about. What is the most significant idea you have learned for your own quiet time? What discipline of devotion will you begin experimenting with in your quiet time?

MY RESPONSE:

Day Twenty-Six

WHEN YOU LOSE YOUR QUIET TIME

In the world you will have tribulation,
but take courage, I have overcome the world.

JOHN 16:33

⁓∞⤳

imes of trouble are opportunities for intimacy with God. In times of suffering, you may lose your quiet time. Jesus said, "In the world you will have tribulation, but take courage, I have overcome the world" (John 16:33). These difficult times can deepen your relationship with the Lord if you will simply draw near to Him. Trials, tribulations, and transitions are the tools that God uses to bring about more intimacy in your relationship with Him.

I heard a panicked voice on the other end of the phone telling me things I did not want to hear. My mother had fallen during the night, and paramedics were rushing her to the hospital. The neighbor relaying the news broke down, sobbing into the receiver. Later at the hospital, we learned the serious extent of the injury—a fracture of the cervical vertebrae. My mother was fortunate to be alive. Waves of fear and uncertainty swept over me, dulling my senses. How could this happen? Who knows the future?

Dramatic changes in your life challenge your desire to spend time with God. These changes include times of trial, times of tribulation, or simply times of transition. Fear, uncertainty, and even apathy may take control of your mind and emotions. Rather than seeking the Lord in earnest and fervent quiet times, you may actually feel like running away from Him. This results in a loss of intimate fellowship with God. In essence, you lose your quiet time.

Although the Christian's positional relationship with God never changes, his or her intimacy with Him can vary with attitudes and emotions. Transitions such as starting a new job or moving into a new house may disrupt your routine. Trials such as marriage conflicts or losing your job serve to test your faith. Tribulation such as serious illness or financial ruin can usher you into suffering a dark night of the soul. And perhaps, without even realizing it, you distance yourself from God just as Adam hid himself in the Garden of Eden and the people of Israel did in the time of Jeremiah.

Around 597 BC, the people of Israel had moved from intimacy with God to a place where they had totally forgotten about the Lord. They were still God's people, but they were living as though God did not even exist. So God sent His people into exile in the land of Babylon under the rule of Nebuchadnezzar. The Israelites faced culture shock, despair, and hopelessness. No future. No hope. All was lost.

During this time, Jeremiah, God's prophet, wrote a dynamic letter to the people of Israel that included these words:

> "Build houses and live in them; and plant gardens and eat their produce. Take wives and become the fathers of sons and daughters, and take wives for your sons and give your daughters to husbands, that they may bear sons and daughters; and multiply there and do not decrease. Seek the welfare of the city where I have sent you into exile, and pray to the Lord on its behalf…For I know the plans that I have for you," declares the Lord, "plans for welfare and not for

calamity to give you a future and a hope. Then you will call upon Me and come and pray to Me, and I will listen to you. You will seek Me and find Me when you search for Me with all your heart" (Jeremiah 29:5-7,11-13).

In these words, God told His people what He wanted them to *know* and what He wanted them to *do* during times of trial, tribulation, and transition.

WHAT GOD WANTS YOU TO KNOW

What does God want you to *know* in times of trial, tribulation, or transition? These truths are designed to give you hope.

God wants you to know *He knows*. He says, "For I know the plans I have for you." Even if you don't understand what is going on, God knows. My Dad sent me an e-mail one day with this thought: "Isn't it amazing that there is not one thing that God doesn't know? He knows everything!" God knows the plans He has for you. You don't have to know all the details because He knows them. Isn't that a comfort? This attribute is known as the omniscience of God. Listen to what A.W. Tozer says about God's omniscience in his book *The Knowledge of the Holy:*

> To say that God is omniscient is to say that He possesses perfect knowledge and therefore has no need to learn...God perfectly knows Himself and, being the source and author of all things, it follows that He knows all that can be known. And this He knows instantly and with a fullness of perfection that includes every possible item of knowledge concerning everything that exists or could have existed anywhere in the universe at any time in the past or that may exist in the centuries or ages yet unborn...God knows instantly and effortlessly all causes, all thoughts, all mysteries, all enigmas, all feeling, all desires, every unuttered secret, all thrones and dominions, all personalities, all things visible and invisible in heaven and in earth, motion, space, time, life, death, good, evil, heaven...He is never surprised, never amazed.[1]

The great comfort, Tozer says, is that nothing can come to light that would turn God away from us, since He knew us utterly before we knew Him and called us to Himself in the full knowledge of everything that was against us. Because of Jesus, His knowledge of our afflictions and adversities is more than theoretical; it is personal, warm, and compassionate. Whatever may befall us, God knows and cares as no one else can.

This realization was of tremendous encouragement to the people of Israel because it assured them that God had not abandoned them—not even in exile in Babylon. You can be encouraged to know that He has not abandoned you. He will never leave or forsake you. God wants you to know He knows, so you don't have to worry or be anxious. Jesus said, "Do not worry about tomorrow; for tomorrow will care for itself. Each day has enough trouble of its own" (Matthew 6:34). The fact that God knows becomes an extremely powerful truth when you discover what He knows: "I know the plans I have for you."

God wants you to know *He has a plan for you.* God is always at work, even now, right where you are in the midst of your trial. What an encouragement to the people of Israel to know that God's plan still included them—even in Babylon. Their suffering was not pointless. Paul encouraged the suffering Philippian church that God was at work in them both to will and to work for His good pleasure (Philippians 2:13). God would bring that work to completion. Regardless of what you've done or what trials you are experiencing, you can never run away from the purposes of God.

God wants you to know *His plan for you is good.* What a reason to hope! Circumstances may not necessarily be pleasant or happy or painless, but God is always working out His good plan and purpose. He says through Jeremiah, "I know the plans that I have for you… plans for welfare and not for calamity, to give you a future and a hope" (Jeremiah 29:11). Even in the midst of adversity, God can work out His good plan.

God wants you to know *He has a future for you.* Paul refers to "things which eye has not seen and ear has not heard, and which have not entered the heart of man, all that God has prepared for those who love Him" (1 Corinthians 2:9). To experience God's future, let go of the past. Paul says, "Forgetting what lies behind and reaching forward to what lies ahead, I press on toward the goal for the prize of the upward call of God in Christ Jesus" (Philippians 3:13-14). The "what-ifs" and "if onlys" of the past can paralyze you in the present. Let go of the past in order to embrace the plan of God.

God wants you to know *He has a hope for you.* The phrase "a future and a hope" in the Hebrew literally means "an end and a hope," which is a figure of speech that means "a hopeful end." Sometimes I think to myself in the midst of a very difficult trial, *What good is my hope? When are God's promises going to be fulfilled?* Paul describes the nature of our hope in Romans 8:23-25 (NLT):

> Even we Christians, although we have the Holy Spirit within us as a foretaste of future glory, also groan to be released from pain and suffering. We, too, wait anxiously for that day when God will give us our full rights as his children, including the new bodies he has promised us. Now that we are saved, we eagerly look forward to this freedom. For if you already have something, you don't need to hope for it. But if we look forward to something we don't have yet, we must wait patiently and confidently.

In the Greek, the word for "patiently" is *hupomone* and means "the spirit which can bear things, not simply with resignation but with blazing hope. It is not the patience which grimly waits for the end, but the patience which radiantly hopes for the dawn."[2]

WHAT GOD WANTS YOU TO DO

God may choose to be silent during trials, tribulations, and transitions, placing you in the "wait patiently" mode. In the case of the Israelites in Babylon, God told His people what to do, giving us wisdom to take to our hearts as well.

God wants us to *build and plant where we are.* For the Israelites, their exile was going to last 70 years. God told them to "Build houses and settle down; plant gardens and eat what they produce" (Jeremiah 29:5 NIV). They were to live in the present and forget the past. He desired that they open their hand to Him where they were and receive life from Him there. When God brought change to their lives, whether they considered it good or bad, they were to open their eyes to His will. The underlying attitude was one of submission to the Lord's hand in their lives.

I often think of Corrie Ten Boom and her sister, imprisoned in Ravensbruck concentration camp during World War II. It could have been so easy for the sisters to wallow in despair, but they recognized that even in prison God had entrusted a ministry to them. As they shared God's Word, the gospel, and carried on Bible studies, many found the Lord. They learned the secret of building and planting where they were.

I also think of Amy Carmichael, one of my great heroes. A missionary in India, she lived there almost her entire life, writing spiritual works including *The Edges of His Ways, Thou Givest...They Gather*, and *Gold by Moonlight*. What many do not know about Amy Carmichael is that she suffered a crippling accident and spent the last 20 years of her life in bed. She wrote many of her books during this time. She was well acquainted with suffering, but God gave her a powerful ministry. Amy learned the secret of building and planting where God had placed her. God was present with Amy even in her bed of suffering.

God is present and at work with you where you are in your life. Regardless of how dramatic the changes, God has a plan. Be open to it. Build and plant where you are. How are you handling change in your life? Maybe you have an affliction that seems to weigh you down. Maybe your life responsibilities are changing. Maybe you or your spouse has lost a job and you are facing financial trouble. Maybe you have been forced to sell your house and move. Regardless of your situation, ask God how you can build and plant where He has placed you. This will require adaptation and endurance.

God wants us to *pray in our present situation*. God said to the people of Israel, "Seek the peace and prosperity of the city to which I have carried you into exile. Pray to the LORD for it, because if it prospers, you too will prosper" (Jeremiah 29:7 NIV). Become a prayer warrior. In a time of change, you may be tempted to put your devotional life, your life of prayer, on hold until you become more stable. But prayer stabilizes you, keeping you from becoming bitter and resentful. Prayer can become the fuel to take your quiet time with the Lord to new depths.

What does God ultimately intend as the result of trial, tribulation, and transition in your life? What is the desired outcome? God says in Jeremiah 29:12-14 (NIV), "'Then you will call upon me and come and pray to me, and I will listen to you. You will seek me and find me when you seek me with all your heart. I will be found by you,' declares the Lord, 'and will bring you back from captivity.'" In the present, you will experience a deeper intimacy with God. As Christians we have the ultimate future and hope. Someday our faith is going to be made sight. All the clouds will be rolled back as a scroll. The trump shall resound and the Lord shall descend. And it will be well with our soul. Jesus Christ is coming again. Someday we are going to see Him face-to-face, and we will step from time into eternity. That is our future. And that is our hope.

My Response

DATE:

KEY VERSE: "In the world you will have tribulation, but take courage; I have overcome the world" (John 16:33).

FOR FURTHER THOUGHT: How do trials, tribulations, and transitions impact a life? Have you experienced any such suffering in recent days? Describe your response to these events. How do the words of Jesus in John 16:33 encourage you today? How is your fellowship with the Lord? Do you need to let go of anything in the past? And what ideas for your future do you need to let go of in order to embrace the plan of God in the present? Write your responses in the space below.

MY RESPONSE:

Day Twenty-Seven

SHAKE UP YOUR QUIET TIME

This is the day the LORD has made,
let us rejoice and be glad in it.

PSALM 118:24 NIV

Quiet time is an opportunity for a new beginning each day. Paul said, "Forgetting what lies behind, and reaching forward to what lies ahead, I press on toward the goal" (Philippians 3:13-14). The psalmist said, "This is the day the LORD has made, let us rejoice and be glad in it" (Psalm 118:24 NIV). But how do you restore your fellowship with God through your quiet time? What can you do to "shake up" your quiet time by making dramatic changes to your routine?

- *Find a new devotional book.* Search the devotional reading list in appendix 4 for a book that will challenge your ideas, attitudes, and thought processes.

- *Change your Bible reading plan.* Focus on your specific trial, tribulation, or transition. If your faith is being tested, find a Bible study on faith. If you are facing serious illness, search for a study on hope. If you lose your favorite quiet place because of a major transition, find a study on peace.

- *Join a new Bible study group.* Meet new friends who will encourage you in your time of change.

- *Write out Scripture.* Immerse yourself in the Psalms. Compare and contrast multiple translations, word for word, in your journal.

- *Memorize Scripture.* Absorb Philippians or another book of the Bible. Recite the Scripture to yourself throughout the day.

- *Be extravagant with God's Word.* Go overboard with a new Bible study tool, such as a commentary or concordance, and live in a passage.

- *Dedicate daily journal and prayer pages.* Focus entirely on your present situation.

- *Sing in your quiet time.* Get a hymnal or Christian songbook and begin singing out loud. Write your own psalm and sing it to the Lord.

- *Embrace intentional devotion by faith.* Intentionally pursue time with the Lord in spite of your trial, tribulation, and transition. Give yourself a quiet time break.

- *Pray about your quiet time.* Expect Him to answer!

Many years ago, the Duke of Wellington led English forces against Napoleon in a critical battle near Waterloo, Belgium. All of England waited eagerly for the first news from the returning warships. Atop Winchester Cathedral, signal flags began to spell out the eagerly awaited message. A dense fog rolled into London just as the words "Wellington defeated" were completed. The heartbreaking news of Wellington's defeat spread throughout London. Before long, the fog lifted and the signal flags atop the cathedral became visible, this time spelling out the complete message: "Wellington defeated the enemy." What a great lesson! Don't be so quick to judge trials, tribulations, and transitions in your life as doom and gloom. Don't allow the dense fog of change to keep you from spending time with the Lord. And don't allow adverse circumstances to prevent you from seeing God's message to you: "For I know the plans that I have for you...plans for welfare and not for calamity to give you a future and a hope" (Jeremiah 29:11). Give God time and let the fog lift, and you will see great reason to hope again.

Father, it is true that we see through a glass darkly in this life, but someday we will see You face-to-face. Thank You, Lord, that You know us—our past, present, and future—and that You love us. Lord, give us the faith to believe Your Word, the strength to stand strong in Your truth, and the courage to march forward as soldiers of Christ. In Jesus' name. Amen.

My Response

DATE:

KEY VERSE: "'For I know the plans that I have for you,' declares the LORD, 'plans for welfare and not for calamity to give you a future and a hope'" (Jeremiah 29:11).

FOR FURTHER THOUGHT: In what way do you need to shake up your quiet time? What idea would you like to implement in your time with the Lord that will change the way you spend time with Him?

MY RESPONSE:

Day Twenty-Eight

CATCH A GLIMPSE OF
THE SPECTACULAR

*Things which eye has not seen, ear has
not heard, and which have not entered
the heart of man, all that God has
prepared for those who love Him.*

I CORINTHIANS 2:9

Radical intimacy opens your life to the spectacular. Paul quotes Isaiah in 1 Corinthians 2:9 regarding "things which eye has not seen, ear has not heard, and which have not entered the heart of man, all that God has prepared for those who love Him." These spectacular experiences that Paul and Isaiah allude to are only open to those who are willing to share the heart of God through much quiet time alone with Him.

One Saturday night a few years ago I collapsed into bed, thoroughly exhausted after a hectic day, falling asleep instantly. Hours later,

I suddenly awoke, remembering that this was to be the night of the largest meteor shower in my lifetime. I leaped out of bed, threw on some clothes, grabbed a blanket, flew through the back door, and embraced the chill of the cold night. My eyes scanned the heavens searching for flashes of light. I saw one shooting star, then another, then two more. I put the blanket down on the pavement and lay flat on my back so I could see the entire sky as one panoramic canvas. For about 15 minutes, nothing happened. I was afraid I had missed the entire event. Still, I waited patiently.

Then, without warning, the real show began. Meteors streamed across the sky in all directions, huge balls of flaming fire with lingering tails trailing behind them. What a show the Lord put on for me!

As I was lying on the pavement, I reflected on how similar this experience was to intimacy with the Lord. Your quiet time brings opportunities to see the spectacular, but it takes patience, endurance, trust, and hope.

- *Patience*—"Follow the example of those who are going to inherit God's promises because of their faith and patience" (Hebrews 6:12 NLT). The stars did not shoot through the sky at my command but had their appointed time. God's timing is not our own; He knows when He wants to give us a glimpse of His heart.

- *Endurance*—"Patient endurance is what you need now... Then you will receive all that he has promised" (Hebrews 10:36 NLT). I fought sleep, doubt, and the chill of the night because I wanted to see the stars more than I wanted my own comfort. Endurance will keep you faithful in quiet time even with the ebb and flow of emotion.

- *Trust*—"And those who know Your name will put their trust in You" (Psalm 9:10). I trusted that I was going to see the stars. Trust keeps you hanging on to every word of God, seeking a glimpse of God Himself.

- *Hope*—"There is a bringing in of a better hope, through which we draw near to God" (Hebrews 7:19). I placed hope in the news reports promising the greatest meteor shower in a lifetime. Our hope is the anchor of our soul, fixed on an extraordinary God and the fulfillment of His promises.

Hosea was a prophet of the Lord, an intimate who shared God's heart. However, he was married to a woman named Gomer, who was unfaithful, just like the people of Israel. In those days, Gomer's actions of adultery were punishable by death, and yet Hosea still loved his wife. What was Hosea to do? God said to Hosea, "Go again, love...an adulteress, even as the Lord loves the sons of Israel, though they turn to other gods and love raisin cakes" (Hosea 3:1). Hosea chose the journey to the heart of God rather than the path of rebellion. As a result, he saw a glimpse of God's heart, a glimpse of the spectacular.

What does it mean to share God's heart—to catch a glimpse of the spectacular?

You will share God's motives. In your quiet time alone with Him, you are going to find that your motives change. As you share His heart, you begin to love—truly love—other people; you discover a love in your heart for those who have mistreated you. God saw His people lusting after raisin cakes, delicacies offered to Baal in thanksgiving for the harvest. Instead of realizing that their protection and blessing came from God, His people gave credit to an idol. How many times in our life do we think the answer is in success, money, a new job, a new relationship, a new body, a new house, or new furniture—the raisin cakes of life?

You will share His message. Hosea 1:2 says "the LORD...spoke through Hosea." God gave Hosea a message to share with His people. Your life can be a message to others as you spend quiet time alone with Him and share the heart of God. Certain Scripture passages transform your thoughts and actions, speaking volumes to those around you.

You will share His mercies. In Hosea 2:14 (AMP), God says about His people: "I will allure her [Israel] and bring her into the wilderness, and I will speak tenderly and to her heart." God's mercies break down the walls of a hard heart, bitterness, sin, grief, and anger. God told Hosea to go get Gomer and not leave her in her miserable choice.

You will share His ministry. Hosea had a ministry that lasted 58 years as a prophet of doom to the northern kingdom. "Listen to the word of the LORD, O sons of Israel, for the LORD has a case against the inhabitants of the land" (Hosea 4:1). Hosea shared in the plan and purpose of God.

You will share His meekness. Here was Hosea, faithful to the Lord, living in the midst of an unfaithful people, and married to an unfaithful woman. Hosea humbled himself to the point that he rescued Gomer, "a woman who is loved by her husband" (Hosea 3:1) in spite of her unfaithfulness. Meekness is your great strength, implying that you draw your strength from God, not from people, things, or circumstances.

You will share His majesty. By faith, Hosea experienced the majesty of God. "The word of the LORD...came to Hosea" (Hosea 1:1) and "When the LORD first spoke through Hosea" (Hosea 1:2) speak of the awesome majesty of God revealed to one of His servants.

You will share His music. He gave Hosea His song—a song of joy and praise. You can hear this music of praise in Hosea 6:3, "Let us know, let us press on to know the LORD. His going forth is as certain as the dawn," as well as in the last verse of Hosea's prophecy (Hosea 14:9): "the ways of the LORD are right, and the righteous will walk in them."

You will share His moves. In the midst of his own pain and heartbreak, Hosea caught a glimpse of the spectacular as he danced with the Lord. He was able to say to the people of Israel, "Come, let us return to the LORD. For He has torn us, but He will heal us; He has wounded us, but He will bandage us. He will revive us after two days; He will raise us up on the third day, that we may live before Him" (Hosea 6:1-2).

> There is a place of quiet rest,
> Near to the heart of God;
> A place where sin cannot molest,
> Near to the heart of God.
>
> There is a place of comfort sweet,
> Near to the heart of God;
> A place where we our Savior meet,
> Near to the heart of God.
>
> There is a place of full release,
> Near to the heart of God;
> A place where all is joy and peace,
> Near to the heart of God.

O Jesus, blest Redeemer,
Sent from the heart of God,
Hold us who wait before Thee
Near to the heart of God.

Cleland McAfee

My Response

DATE:

KEY VERSE: "No eye has seen, no ear has heard, and no mind has imagined what God has prepared for those who love him" (1 Corinthians 2:9 NLT).

FOR FURTHER THOUGHT: What is the most exciting truth you've learned about God and His ways in the last year? Will you write a prayer today, thanking Him for who He is?

MY RESPONSE:

Day Twenty-Nine

THE LIFE OF RADICAL INTIMACY

I urge you, brethren, by the mercies of God, to present your bodies a living and holy sacrifice, acceptable to God, which is your spiritual service of worship.

ROMANS 12:1

Radical intimacy knows a radical commitment. Paul said, "I urge you, brethren, by the mercies of God, to present your bodies a living and holy sacrifice, acceptable to God, which is your spiritual service of worship" (Romans 12:1). What does it mean to be radically intimate with God? It means I have laid everything on the altar. I will not look back. I will not turn back. For me, the decision has been made. I am His disciple. I will go where He leads me, and I will give my all. I will live my life on the edge of my faith.

As a young man, Jim Elliot dreamed of taking the gospel to the Auca Indians in the heart of the jungle in Ecuador. Ready and willing to sacrifice all for Christ, he wrote in his journal, "He is no fool who gives up what he cannot keep, to gain what he cannot lose." Years later, while working with the Quichua Indians in Ecuador, Jim was quietly planning a strategy to reach the Auca Indians, who were known to be ruthless killers. After three months of dropping gifts from the plane to this remote tribe of Indians, Jim and his crew finally landed on a small stretch of beach along the Curaray River. Three days later, Auca Indians came to the beach seemingly hungry for friendship, but on Sunday, January 8, 1956, in the early afternoon, a group of ten Aucas attacked Jim Elliot and his fellow missionaries with wooden spears and killed them all. In a diary entry, Jim had written, "God, I pray Thee, light these idle sticks of my life, that I may burn for Thee. Consume my life, my God, for it is Thine. I seek not a long life, but a full one, like You, Lord Jesus."

God does not call every saint to a martyr's death like Jim Elliot's. But He does call us to the kind of commitment that was apparent in Jim Elliot's life. Jim Elliot was a radical disciple, recklessly abandoned to the will of God and wholeheartedly devoted to Jesus Christ.

WHAT DOES RADICAL INTIMACY LOOK LIKE IN YOUR LIFE?

Radical intimacy knows a *radical relationship* with Jesus Christ. A radical relationship means that knowing Him is more important than anything else. Paul, an intimate of the Lord, called knowing Christ a "priceless privilege" (Philippians 3:8 Williams New Testament). Do you count knowing Christ as a priceless privilege? Where do you spend your time? What fills your mind and heart? What occupies your plans and your datebook each day? Look at your checkbook—where do you spend your money? A radical intimacy sets aside the things of this world to enter into the priceless privilege of knowing Christ.

Radical intimacy knows a *radical commitment*. Paul said, "I can do all things through Christ who strengthens me" (Philippians 4:13 NKJV). Nothing stopped Paul. Why? Because nothing stopped Jesus. Jesus said, "Here on earth you will have many trials and sorrows. But take heart, because I have overcome the world" (John 16:33 NLT). Paul says in 2 Corinthians 4:1 (NLT), "Since God in his mercy has given us this wonderful ministry, we never give up." Have you lost your hope? Do you feel weak? Do you feel defeated by circumstances, as though you cannot win? A radical intimacy never gives up because of the overcoming spirit of the Lord Jesus Christ running through the spiritual veins and heart of that disciple.

Radical intimacy knows a *radical contentment.* Paul said, "I have learned the secret of being content in any and every situation" (Philippians 4:12 NIV). Are you willing to accomplish the lowliest task, do the most humble job, or love the unlovely? A radical intimacy is willing to live in obscurity because the only audience that is necessary is God Himself.

Radical intimacy knows a *radical faith.* "And this is the victory that has overcome the world—our faith. Who is he who overcomes the world, but he who believes that Jesus is the Son of God?" (1 John 5:4-5 NKJV). Are you living a radical faith that overcomes the world? Do you walk by faith, or do you walk by sight (2 Corinthians 5:7)? A radical intimacy is motivated by the truth of God's Word.

Radical intimacy knows a *radical purpose.* Paul said, "I do all things for the sake of the gospel" (1 Corinthians 9:23). That goal ran his life. Are you clear about your goal and purpose in life? Have you sought God for a life verse? A radical intimacy traces all decisions to a single-minded purpose and calling from God.

Radical intimacy knows a *radical ministry.* Paul said, "The things which you have heard from me in the presence of many witnesses, entrust these to faithful men who will be able to teach others also" (2 Timothy 2:2). Dr. Henrietta Mears became Director of Christian Education at First Presbyterian Church in Hollywood, California, in 1928. During her tenure, Sunday school attendance grew from 400 to 4000. Frustrated by the limited Bible study curriculum, she wrote all the lessons herself, driven by her passion to teach the Word of God. Inspired by her ministry, more than 400 young people entered full-time Christian service, including Dr. Bill Bright, founder of Campus Crusade for Christ, Richard Halverson, chaplain of the Senate, and

Billy Graham. Her influence stretched far and wide with the founding of Gospel Light Publications and the Forest Home retreat center. "Only one life, 'twill soon be past; only what's done for Christ will last." A radical intimacy influences the world for Jesus Christ.

May our words echo the words of the young pastor from Zimbabwe, Africa, who was martyred for his faith in Jesus Christ. This note was found in his office following his martyrdom:

> I'm part of the fellowship of the unashamed. I have the Holy Spirit's power. The die has been cast. I have stepped over the line. The decision has been made—I'm a disciple of His. I won't look back, let up, slow down, back away, or be still. My past is redeemed, my present makes sense, my future is secure. I'm finished and done with low living, sight walking, smooth knees, colorless dreams, tamed visions, worldly talking, cheap giving, and dwarfed goals.
>
> I no longer need preeminence, prosperity, position, promotions, plaudits, or popularity. I don't have to be right, first, tops, recognized, praised, regarded, or rewarded. I now live by faith, lean in His presence, walk by patience, am uplifted by prayer, and I labor with power.
>
> My face is set, my gait is fast, my goal is heaven, my road is narrow, my way rough, my companions are few, my Guide reliable, my mission clear. I cannot be bought, compromised, detoured, lured away, turned back, deluded, or delayed. I will not flinch in the face of sacrifice, hesitate in the presence of the enemy, pander at the pool of popularity, or meander in the maze of mediocrity.
>
> I won't give up, shut up, let up, until I have stayed up, stored up, prayed up, paid up, preached up for the cause of Christ. I am a disciple of Jesus. I must go till He comes, give till I drop, preach till all know, and work till He stops me. And, when He comes for His own, He will have no problem recognizing me...my banner will be clear![1]

"My banner will be clear." Those are the words of a true disciple of Jesus Christ. May his tribe increase! One who knows radical intimacy with God is, as Tozer says, facing one direction only, has stopped looking back, and has no further plans of his own. The world has yet to see what

God can do in and through the life of one who is wholly committed to Him. May you be that one who will know radical intimacy with the Lord. Someday you and I will stand before our Lord. Oh, how wonderful it will be for you as you look into His eyes and hear His Words to you: "Well done, good and faithful servant." Then you will know it was worth it all. God bless you, dear friend. Keep running the race and fix your eyes on Jesus!

My Response

DATE:

KEY VERSE: "Therefore I urge you, brethren, by the mercies of God, to present your bodies a living and holy sacrifice, acceptable to God, which is your spiritual service of worship" (Romans 12:1).

FOR FURTHER THOUGHT: What does it mean to be radically intimate with the Lord? As you think about all the qualities of one who is radical in his or her intimacy with God, which quality appeals to you the most right now? Will you close by writing a prayer expressing your desire for radical intimacy with your Lord?

MY RESPONSE:

Day Thirty

QUIET TIME—
WEEK FIVE:
ENJOY THE VIEW

I love you, O LORD, my strength.

∾

PREPARE YOUR HEART

As you finish your 30-day journey to discover radical intimacy with God, it is time to think about your own life and relationship with the Lord. The real question is, what will you do with what you have learned? Will you draw near to God and know and enjoy Him? With this book, you have discovered numerous resources to help you on your journey. Your decisions now about quiet time will influence your entire life and the lives of those around you. The world has yet to see what God can do in and through the lives of those who are wholly committed to Him. You can know this: Every moment spent with the Lord in His Word and in prayer will result in transformed lives. No time is ever wasted when it is time spent with God. One of our greatest examples is Charles

Haddon Spurgeon, often called the "prince of preachers," who lived in the 1800s. Spurgeon was extremely popular in his day. However, what many do not realize is that he experienced many troubling times that drove him to bouts of depression. The answer for him was to "get away" with God. He was known for his intimate devotional life. Not only did he know the Bible well, but he would read six devotional books a week. He owned at least 6000 volumes of Puritan writings and was well-versed in their deep thoughts. Spurgeon's practice of getting away with God allowed him to write weekly sermons that were published and read by thousands. Who knows—perhaps the influence of your life will be the influence of a Charles Haddon Spurgeon, an A.W. Tozer, or an Amy Carmichael. Maybe you will be like Oswald Chambers, whose influence grew only after his death when his wife took the notes from his lectures and transformed them into books and devotionals, including *My Utmost for His Highest.* Or you may be an Octavius Winslow, who lived during the time of Spurgeon and was faithful to the Lord, influencing many in his time. You be responsible for the depth of your ministry and let God be responsible for the breadth of your ministry. As you grow intimate with the Lord, He will be the One to determine the length and breadth of the influence of your life. And you may only see it in heaven. May you be famous in the courts of heaven, for that is where you want to be known and loved—at the throne of God.

As you begin the final quiet time in this series, turn to the words of David in Psalm 27. Record your most significant insight in the space provided.

READ AND STUDY GOD'S WORD

1. David, the man after God's own heart, was probably one of the greatest radical intimates of all time. Read his words in Psalm 18:1-19 and record what David knew about God.

2. How would you describe David's relationship with the Lord from what you have seen in Psalm 18:1-19?

3. What is your favorite insight about God from Psalm 18:1-19?

4. How would you describe your own relationship with the Lord?

ADORE GOD IN PRAYER

Use the words of David's Psalm 18:1-3 as your prayer today:

I love You, O LORD, my strength.
The LORD is my rock and my fortress and my deliverer,
My God, my rock, in whom I take refuge;
My shield and the horn of my salvation, my stronghold.
I call upon the LORD, who is worthy to be praised,
And I am saved from my enemies.

YIELD YOURSELF TO GOD

Read the following words by Spurgeon on the great value of knowing God:

Every believer understands that to know God is the highest and best form of knowledge; and this spiritual knowledge is a source of strength to the Christian. It strengthens his *faith*. Believers are constantly spoken of in the Scriptures as being persons who are enlightened and taught of the Lord; they are said to "have an unction from the Holy One," and it is the Spirit's peculiar office to lead them into all truth, and all this for the increase and the fostering of their faith. Knowledge strengthens *love*, as well as faith. Knowledge opens the door, and then through that door we see our Saviour. Or, to use another similitude, knowledge paints the portrait of Jesus, and when we see that portrait then we love him. We cannot love a Christ whom we do not know, at least, in some degree. If we know but little of the excellencies of Jesus, what he has done for us, and what he is doing now, we cannot love him much; but the more we know him, the more we shall love him. Knowledge also strengthens *hope*. How can we hope for a thing if we do not know of its existence? Hope may be the telescope, but till we receive instruction, our ignorance stands in the front of the glass, and we can see nothing whatever; knowledge removes the interposing object, and when we look through the bright optic glass we discern the glory to be revealed, and anticipate it with joyous confidence. Knowledge supplies us reasons for *patience*. How shall we have patience unless we know something of the sympathy of Christ, and understand the good which is to come out of the correction which our heavenly Father sends us? Nor is there one single grace of the Christian which, under God, will not be fostered and brought to perfection by holy knowledge. How important, then, is it that we should grow not only in grace, but in the "knowledge" of our Lord and Saviour Jesus Christ.[1]

Charles Haddon Spurgeon
Morning and Evening

ENJOY HIS PRESENCE

On Day 1 you had the opportunity to write a letter to the Lord in response to His invitation to intimacy. Read through your letter and think about all you have learned. How will what you have learned change the way you will spend time with God in the future? How has God worked in your life as you have read this book? What is the most significant truth you have learned? What is one idea that has made a difference in your quiet time? Please know that I am praying for you. Whenever you need encouragement in your quiet time, pick up this book again and read those chapters where you need the challenge and inspiration. To continue on and put these truths to practice, I encourage you to grab one of the books of quiet times, *Pilgrimage of the Heart, Revive My Heart!, A Heart That Dances, A Heart on Fire,* or *A Heart to See Forever,* and begin spending time with the Lord. God bless you as you continue on in the great adventure of knowing God. Close your time by writing a prayer to the Lord, expressing all that is on your heart.

REST IN HIS LOVE

"I count all things to be loss in view of the surpassing value of knowing Christ Jesus my Lord, for whom I have suffered the loss of all things, and count them but rubbish so that I may gain Christ" (Philippians 3:8).

Appendix 1

DISCUSSION
QUESTIONS

These questions are designed to be used in a group to share the journey together. This book is a great tool for talking together about how to have a quiet time. It also provides for a great 30-day campaign experience prior to beginning one of the books of quiet times available from Quiet Time Ministries *(Pilgrimage of the Heart, Revive My Heart!, A Heart That Dances, A Heart on Fire,* and *A Heart to See Forever).* You are free to use these questions and as a leader, you will probably add to them with questions the Lord puts on your heart to help others discover the great adventure of knowing God. God bless you.

INTRODUCTION

The introduction week is designed to meet those in your group, hand out this book to each participant, familiarize everyone with the topic of quiet time, and play the "Introduction Message" (if you are using the weekly DVD messages for *Six Secrets to a Powerful Quiet Time*). A good question to begin your group time is this: "What brought you to this 30-day journey of *Six Secrets to a Powerful Quiet Time*? How did you hear about it?" Allow everyone to share. Then pass out the books and show those in your group how each week is organized according to six days with a quiet time as the sixth day. Show your group all the information in the appendixes. Tell them about the websites www.radicalintimacy.com and www.quiettime.org and the message boards where they may share insights online with others. Then describe how you will meet weekly and will discuss your insights, followed by a DVD message (if you're using the weekly DVD messages for *Six Secrets to a Powerful Quiet Time*). You may want to use a signup sheet for snacks. Close in prayer.

WEEK ONE DISCUSSION QUESTIONS—THE GREAT ADVENTURE

Day 1—*The Invitation to Radical Intimacy*

1. Begin your time together in prayer. What did you experience by spending daily time thinking about your quiet time with the Lord?

2. After reading through all the days in this first week, how would you describe radical intimacy? What does it mean?

3. What was your favorite statement in Day 1 about the invitation to radical intimacy? What challenged you? What encouraged you?

4. Why do you think making a commitment to know God is important in experiencing radical intimacy?

5. Consider the importance of the prayer to receive Christ in the Response section of Day 1. If you have prayed that prayer, you have forgiveness of sins and eternal life, and you are beginning a great adventure of knowing God.

Day 2—*The Path to Radical Intimacy*

1. This day begins with these statements: "God has a message to write on your heart. When your heart dances with the

Lord, the dance tells a story to the world. It's the story of your life with Him. That's why knowing God is such an adventure." What can you share from your adventure with the Lord? What is the story of your life with Him? What has He been teaching you these days?

2. What encouraged you the most from Day 2?

Day 3—The Goal of Radical Intimacy

1. Why is knowing your goal so important in the journey to radical intimacy?

2. What kinds of things are necessary to achieve goals in life? What attitudes and actions will help us achieve goals?

3. Has God given you a life goal and a life verse that you would like to share with everyone?

4. There are many benefits of pursuing the goal listed in Day 3. Which benefit means the most to you right now in your own life?

Day 4—The Quiet Time Plan: Where Do I Begin?

1. What is your favorite time to spend with the Lord?

2. How has quiet time made a difference in your days?

3. What is your favorite quiet place?

4. What part of the P.R.A.Y.E.R. Quiet Time Plan do you feel you need to focus the most on at this time in your life?

5. Was there a favorite quote in Day 4 that encourages you?

Day 5—The Grand Experiment: Quiet Time Resources

1. What are your favorite resources in your quiet time?

2. What resources do you want to add to your quiet time?

Day 6—"The Great Adventure" Quiet Time

1. We spent time this week reading *about* quiet time, and then on Day 6 we had the opportunity to *do* quiet time. What did you learn from doing the quiet time? What was your most important insight from the quiet time?

2. What quote, verse, or insight encouraged you the most this week?

WEEK TWO DISCUSSION QUESTIONS—BEGIN THE CLIMB

Day 7—Secret One: Prepare Your Heart

1. Introduce today's discussion by doing a quick review of what you discussed last week. This will be of special benefit to those who are just joining your group. Review the idea that radical intimacy is all about the great adventure of knowing God. It is something that doesn't just happen. It takes time alone with God. To spend time with God each day, it is helpful to set aside a time, choose a place, and have a plan. Last week we talked about what a challenge it is in this culture to actually slow down and leisurely enjoy time with God. That can bring such blessing. Then we talked about special quiet places we've enjoyed with God. And then we introduced the P.R.A.Y.E.R. plan to spend time alone with God. P.R.A.Y.E.R. is an acrostic:

> **P**repare Your Heart
>
> **R**ead and Study God's Word
>
> **A**dore God in Prayer
>
> **Y**ield Yourself to God
>
> **E**njoy His presence
>
> **R**est in His Love

2. Today we want to talk together about the first element of your quiet time, preparing your heart. What do we mean by "preparation" in relation to our quiet time?

3. Why is preparation so important to our quiet time?

Day 8—Simple Prayer, Solitude, and Silence

1. How does simple prayer prepare you to meet alone with the Lord?

2. Do you have a favorite prayer that is simple but that effectively takes your heart to the Lord?

3. What helps you find solitude in your life?

4. What do you think is the value of solitude and silence in growing your relationship with the Lord?

Day 9—Your Journal

1. In Day 9 you had the opportunity to think about journaling. Has journaling been something that you have used in your quiet time, and if so, how has it helped in your own relationship with the Lord?

2. What do you use for your journal?

3. Did you have a favorite quote in this day on journaling?

Day 10—Writing in Your Journal

1. What is your favorite way to write in your journal?

2. What do you think is the greatest benefit of journaling?

Day 11—Christian Meditation

1. In Day 11 you looked at meditation as a preparation for your quiet time. Describe what it means to meditate on God's Word.

2. What is your favorite hymn or worship song to use for Christian meditation?

3. Why do you think music is so effective in preparing your heart to meet alone with the Lord?

4. Do you have a favorite book that you use in your own quiet time?

5. Whose writing has challenged you the most in your relationship with the Lord?

6. What book would you like to add to your quiet time?

7. Did you have a favorite quote in this chapter on Christian meditation?

Day 12—"Begin the Climb" Quiet Time

1. In your quiet time this week on Day 12, what meant the most to you from the example of Robert Murray McCheyne?

2. What did you learn about meditation in "Read and Study God's Word"?

3. What was your most important insight in the quiet time?

4. How did this week's reading influence your life? What was your favorite quote, thought, or verse? What have you thought about most this week as you have begun this 30-day journey of discovering radical intimacy with God?

WEEK THREE DISCUSSION QUESTIONS—EXPLORE THE LANDSCAPE

Day 13—Secret Two: Read and Study God's Word

1. In the last two weeks we have been talking about radical intimacy and what it requires in the life of one who would be intimate with the Lord. We have looked at quiet time and its importance in growing in your relationship with Christ. As we begin today, what is the most important thing you've learned so far in this 30-day journey of quiet time?

2. In Day 13 you looked at another aspect of the P.R.A.Y.E.R. Quiet Time Plan: Read and Study God's Word. Why is the Word of God essential in becoming radically intimate with the Lord?

Day 14—Your Bible Reading Plan

1. In Day 14 we explored the importance of a Bible reading plan. Why is a plan to be in God's Word so vital?

2. What are some of your favorite Bible reading plans?

Day 15—Digging Deeper

1. Day 15 begins this way: "Treasure in God's Word is discovered." What is so exciting about discovery when it involves digging deeper in God's Word?

2. What was the most important idea you learned about digging deeper into God's Word? Was there something that you would like to try in your own quiet time?

3. Have you ever had a time when you cross-referenced a verse or looked up the meaning of a word and it became important to your relationship with the Lord?

4. Why is it important to apply God's Word to your own life?

Day 16—Get Personal

1. What does it mean to personalize the Word of God?

2. Why is it important to personalize Scripture?

3. What are some ways that you have made the Bible your own, a true friend in your relationship with the Lord?

Day 17—My Favorite Bible Study Tools

1. What are some of your favorite Bible study tools?

2. What tool would you like to try in your quiet time?

Day 18—"Explore the Landscape" Quiet Time

1. In Day 18, what meant the most to you from the example of George Mueller?

2. What is the most important truth you learned about the Word of God in Psalm 119 and the other verses?

3. Of everything you've read, what encourages you the most to live in God's Word?

4. What was the most important idea or truth you learned from your time thinking about radical intimacy this week?

WEEK FOUR DISCUSSION QUESTIONS—REACH THE SUMMITS

Day 19—Secret Three: Adore God in Prayer

1. We have been looking these last four weeks at radical intimacy and what it will take to be radically intimate with the Lord. We looked at the importance of a time, a place, and a plan. We've spoken of the importance of preparation in your time alone with the Lord. Then, last week we talked about how to read and study God's Word. Now, we want to share together on the remaining elements of your quiet time plan—Adore God in Prayer, Yield Yourself to God, Enjoy His Presence, and Rest in His Love.

   As you spent this week thinking about these things, what was the most important thing you learned? How did God speak to you this week?

2. Why is prayer important in order for you to be radically intimate with the Lord?

3. What is the most important idea for prayer that you can incorporate into your own quiet time?

4. What is your favorite book on prayer?

Day 20—Secret Four: Yield Yourself to God

1. Why is yielding to God essential to experience radical intimacy?

2. Why is yielding to God so difficult?

3. What mercy of God meant the most to you?

Day 21—A Journey of Surrender

1. What encouraged you in "A Journey of Surrender" on Day 21?

2. Can you think of a time when you have yielded yourself to God? What was the result? What did you learn from this experience?

Day 22—Secret Five: Enjoy His Presence

1. In Day 22 you thought about practicing the presence of God. How have you experienced His presence in your own life?

2. What are some ways that you can cultivate His presence in your own life?

3. Was there an idea that you would like to try in your own relationship with the Lord?

Day 23—Secret Six: Rest in His Love

1. Why does radical intimacy with the Lord result in rest?

2. How can we experience rest?

3. What encouraged you this week that you can share with your group?

Day 24—"Reach the Summits" Quiet Time

1. In your quiet time this week, what did you learn about the importance of prayer in revival?

2. What did you learn about prayer from the example of King Hezekiah?

3. What was your most important insight on prayer from the verses?

4. What was your most important insight from your 30-day journey this week?

WEEK FIVE DISCUSSION QUESTIONS—ENJOY THE VIEW

Day 25—Putting It All Together

1. What a journey we have enjoyed exploring radical intimacy with the Lord. You have spent 30 days focusing on quiet time and, as a result, your devotional life will be more than it has ever been before. This is not really an ending but a beginning as you apply all that you have learned about quiet time. It is important to think about what ideas you would like to implement to enrich your quiet time.

    As you have now finished reading *Six Secrets to a Powerful Quiet Time* what is the most important thing you've learned as a result of the journey? How will this book and its emphasis on quiet time make a difference in your life?

2. In Day 25 you had the opportunity to think about how to put the P.R.A.Y.E.R. Quiet Time Plan together and apply it in your quiet time. Which of the six aspects of the plan is your favorite?

3. How does focus on a detail, a resource, the Lord's leading, or the goal help you in having your quiet time with the Lord (as described in the "Helpful Hints" section of this day)?

Day 26—When You Lose Your Quiet Time

1. In Day 26 we thought about the times in our lives when quiet time becomes very difficult and sometimes even nonexistent. Have you ever had a time when you lost your quiet time?

2. What truth about God has helped you the most or helps you even now in a difficult time?

Day 27—Shake Up Your Quiet Time

1. If you have had a time where you lost your quiet time, what helped you regain it?

2. What idea from Day 27 do you think would be most helpful for regaining quiet time in a difficulty or trial?

Day 28—Catch a Glimpse of the Spectacular

1. Day 28 begins this way: "Radical intimacy opens your life to the spectacular." How have you seen the spectacular in

your relationship with the Lord? How have you seen the spectacular in your quiet time with Him?

2. What kinds of things do you experience when you share God's heart? Can you think of ways that you have shared God's heart?

3. What will it take to catch a glimpse of the spectacular?

Day 29—The Life of Radical Intimacy

1. Why does radical intimacy require commitment? What kind of commitment? What does it look like?

2. What does radical intimacy look like in a person's life?

3. What does it mean to have a radical contentment?

4. What does it mean to have a radical faith?

5. Radical intimacy always influences others. Who has had the most influence in your life?

Day 30—"Enjoy the View" Quiet Time

1. What did you learn from the example of Spurgeon that inspires you in your own life?

2. Why do you think David was a man after God's own heart?

3. As you think about your journey over the last 30 days, what has been most significant to you?

4. What is the most important thing you have learned in this 30-day journey of discovering radical intimacy with God? What will you take with you from this time?

5. Who was your favorite example? What was your favorite verse or favorite quote?

6. Is there anything else you would like to share as a result of your 30-day journey?

7. Close in prayer.

Appendix 2

A QUIET TIME
FOR DETERMINING
YOUR LIFE GOAL
AND LIFE VERSE

PREPARE YOUR HEART

As you begin your time alone with the Lord, draw near to Him by turning to Psalm 34. Meditate on each verse, asking the Lord to teach you during this time alone with Him. Write out one phrase or verse that is significant to you.

READ AND STUDY GOD'S WORD

1. One of the great questions in the Word of God is the one God asked Adam in the Garden of Eden: "Where are you?" As you spend time alone with the Lord, it is good to think through what God has been doing in your life in the last six months. What have you been learning? What is the most significant truth He has taught you from His Word? What has been your trial? What has been your greatest victory?

2. What do you desire in your relationship with the Lord? What would you like to see in terms of spiritual growth?

3. The best way to begin the great adventure of knowing God is to establish a life goal and a life verse. As you think about your life goal and life verse, they should captivate your heart, set your sights, and give you direction for a lifetime. Look up the following verses and record what you learn in the space provided. Be certain to scan the verses before and after these passages to keep their context in mind.

   Jeremiah 9:23-24

1 Chronicles 22:19

2 Chronicles 11:16

Ezra 7:10

Psalm 27:4

Micah 6:8

Deuteronomy 10:12

2 Kings 18:1-6

Acts 13:22

1 Corinthians 9:23-27

Philippians 3:7-11

Matthew 6:33

Hebrews 11:6

4. Summarize what you have learned in two or three sentences.

ADORE GOD IN PRAYER

Ask God to give you a life verse and life goal that will capture your heart for a lifetime.

YIELD YOURSELF TO GOD

1. List several goals derived from what you have learned in the verses you thought about today.

2. Record verses that have been significant to you throughout your life. As you pray for a life verse and daily walk with the Lord, one verse will stand out to you. Once you have a life verse, record it in the space provided.

My Life Verse:

3. Write out a goal derived from the verse that stands out to you the most. Use words that enable you to remember your goal. Record your life goal in the space provided.

My Life Goal:

Enjoy His Presence

As you close this time with the Lord, thank Him for what you have learned. Write out a prayer of thanksgiving expressing the thoughts of your heart. God bless you as you embark on this great adventure of knowing God!

Rest in His Love

"Run in such a way that you may win" (1 Corinthians 9:24).

P.R.A.Y.E.R. QUIET TIME PLAN RESOURCE GUIDE

PREPARE YOUR HEART

- Bible
- Devotionals such as *My Utmost for His Highest, Streams in the Desert, Daily Light*
- Classic Christian books
- Worship, praise, and hymn CDs
- Hymnal
- *Quiet Time Notebook,* journal

READ AND STUDY GOD'S WORD

- Devotional Bibles
- Study Bibles
- Various translations and paraphrases of the Bible

- Bible study tools
- *Quiet Time Notebook*, journal

ADORE GOD IN PRAYER
- Bible
- Prayer books
- Prayer tools such as *Operation World, Praying God's Will, 31 Days of Praise*
- Worship CDs
- *Quiet Time Notebook*, journal

YIELD YOURSELF TO GOD
- Bible
- *Quiet Time Notebook*, journal
- Classic devotional reading

ENJOY HIS PRESENCE
- Bible
- *Quiet Time Notebook*, journal
- Worship CDs

REST IN HIS LOVE
- Bible
- *Quiet Time Notebook*, journal
- Worship CDs

Appendix 4

RECOMMENDED
READING

Between Heaven and Earth by Kenneth Gire (San Francisco: HarperSanFrancisco, 1997).

Celebration of Discipline by Richard J. Foster (San Francisco: Harper & Row, 1988).

The Christian's Secret of a Happy Life by Hannah Whitall Smith (Old Tappan, NJ: Fleming H. Revell Co, 1942).

Chronicles of Narnia by C.S. Lewis (New York: Macmillan, 1953).

Daily Light for Every Day (Nashville: J. Countryman, a division of Thomas Nelson Publishers 1998).

Devotional Classics edited by Richard J. Foster and James Bryan Smith (San Francisco: HarperSan Francisco, 1993). This book is an excellent introduction to devotional classics, providing excerpts from many of the best works.

A Diary of Daily Prayer by John Baillie (London: Oxford University Press, 1936).

Directions for Daily Communion with God by Matthew Henry (Grand Rapids, MI: Baker Book House, 1978).

Discipleship by G. Campbell Morgan (Grand Rapids, MI: Baker Book House, 1973).

The Divine Conquest by A.W. Tozer (Old Tappan, NJ: Fleming H. Revell Company, 1950).

Each New Day by Corrie Ten Boom (Grand Rapids, MI: Fleming H. Revell 1971).

The Edges of His Ways by Amy Carmichael (Fort Washington, PA: Christian Literature Crusade, 1984).

The God of All Comfort by Hannah Whitall Smith (Chicago: Moody Press, 1956).

God's Best Secrets by Andrew Murray (Kregel Publications, 1995).

Gold by Moonlight by Amy Carmichael (Fort Washington, PA: Christian Literature Crusade).

The Green Letters, also titled *Principles of Spiritual Growth* by Miles J. Stanford (Grand Rapids, MI: Zondervan Publishing House, 1975).

Hind's Feet on High Places by Hannah Hurnard (Wheaton, Illinois: Tyndale House Publishers).

How to Pray by R.A. Torrey (Old Tappan, NJ: Fleming H. Revell Company, 1976).

Humility by Andrew Murray (Old Tappan, NJ: Fleming H. Revell Company).

If You Will Ask by Oswald Chambers (Grand Rapids, MI: Discovery House Publishers, 1958).

The Inner Life by Andrew Murray (Grand Rapids, MI: Zondervan, 1980).

The Kneeling Christian, unknown author (Grand Rapids, MI: Zondervan, 1986).

Knowing God by J.I. Packer (Downers Grove, Illinois: InterVarsity Press, 1973).

The Knowledge of the Holy by A.W. Tozer (San Francisco, CA: Harper & Row Publishers, 1961).

Letters of Samuel Rutherford (Carlisle, PA: Banner of Truth, l664–1984).

Letters to Malcolm: Chiefly on Prayer by C.S. Lewis (San Diego, CA: Harcourt Brace Jovanovich Publisher, 1964).

Life Together by Dietrich Bonhoeffer (San Francisco: Harper & Row, 1954).

Luther for the Busy Man compiled by P.D. Pahl (Adelaide: Luther Publishing House, 1974).

The Making of a Man of God: Studies in the Life of David by Alan Redpath (Grand Rapids, Michigan: Fleming H. Revell, 1962).

Man of Prayer by Frank C. Laubach (Syracuse, NY: Laubach Literacy International, 1990).

Memoirs of Robert Murray McCheyne by Andrew Bonar.

Men Who Met God by A.W. Tozer, compiled and edited by Gerald B. Smith (Camp Hill, PA: Christian Publications, 1986).

Morning and Evening by Charles H. Spurgeon (Grand Rapids, MI: Zondervan, 1962).

My Daily Meditation by John Henry Jowett (Published and Distributed by First Church of the Nazarene, 3700 East Sierra Madre Boulevard, Pasadena, California 91107, 626-351-9631, Fifth Printing 1998).

My Utmost for His Highest by Oswald Chambers (Discovery House Publishers 1992). Highly recommended as a daily devotional.

The Necessity of Prayer by E.M. Bounds (New Kensington, PA: Whitaker House, 1984).

The Normal Christian Life by Watchman Nee (Wheaton, IL: Tyndale House Publishers, 1977).

Of the Imitation of Christ by Thomas à Kempis (Grand Rapids, MI: Baker Book House, 1973).

Pilgrim's Progress by John Bunyan (Chicago, IL: Moody Press).

The Power of Extraordinary Prayer by Dr. Robert Bakke (Wheaton, IL: Crossway Books, 2000).

The Power of Prayer in a Believer's Life by Charles Spurgeon (Lynnwood, WA: Emerald Books, 1993).

Power Through Prayer by E.M. Bounds (Grand Rapids, MI: Zondervan Publishing House, 1979).

The Practice of the Presence of God by Brother Lawrence (Springdale, PA: Whitaker House, 1982).

Prayer by O. Hallesby (Minneapolis, MN: Augsburg Publishing House 1931).

Prayer: Finding the Heart's True Home by Richard J. Foster (San Francisco, California: HarperCollins Publishers, 1992).

Psalms: The Prayer Book of the Bible by Dietrich Bonhoeffer (Minneapolis, MN: Augsburg, 1974).

The Pursuit of God by A.W. Tozer (Camp Hill, Pennsylvania: Christian Publications Inc., 1982).

Quiet Talks on Prayer by S.D. Gordon (Fleming H. Revell).

Renewed Day by Day: A Daily Devotional by A.W. Tozer (Camp Hill, Pennsylvania: Christian Publications, Inc., 1950).

Shadow of the Almighty by Elisabeth Elliot (San Francisco, CA: Harper & Row, 1989).

The Spirit of the Disciplines by Dallas Willard (San Francisco: Harper & Row, 1988).

Spiritual Leadership by J. Oswald Sanders (Chicago, IL: Moody Press, 1967).

Springs in the Valley by Mrs. Charles E. Cowman (Grand Rapids, MI: Zondervan Publishing House, 1968).

Thou Givest...They Gather by Amy Carmichael (Fort Washington, PA: Christian Literature Crusade, 1971).

The Valley of Vision: A Collection Of Puritan Prayers and Devotions by Arthur Bennett ed. (Carlisle, PA: Banner Of Truth, 1975).

Waiting on God by Andrew Murray (Chicago, IL: Moody Press).

With Christ in the School of Prayer by Andrew Murray (New-Kensington, PA: Whitaker House, 1981).

WORKSHEET: GETTING STARTED IN YOUR QUIET TIME

1. As you plan for your daily quiet time, spend a few moments evaluating what God has taught you during this past year.

2. What do you desire in your relationship with God? Make a commitment with the Lord to seek Him, know Him, and spend consistent time alone with Him.

3. Choose a time and a place for your quiet time. Organize your quiet time area—keep all your materials together in one place.

Time_____

Place_____

4. Choose some books and daily devotional reading to use as you prepare your heart in your quiet times this year. A list of suggested reading is included in Day 14 of *Six Secrets to a Powerful Quiet Time* or in the introductory section of *The Quiet Time Notebook.*

5. To Read and Study God's Word, decide how you will stay in God's Word on a daily basis this year by choosing a Bible reading plan. Refer to Day 16 in this book or the introductory section of *The Quiet Time Notebook* for different ideas for your Bible reading plan.

6. Evaluate your present devotional materials. Make a list of study tools to obtain in the future as an investment in your relationship with the Lord. The following materials will be helpful in your quiet time: cross-reference Bible, *The Quiet Time Notebook,* devotional reading, cassette recorder/CD

player, praise and worship tapes and CDs, Hebrew-Greek word study Bible, exhaustive concordance.

Bible Study Tools I Have   **Future Bible Study Tools**

7. Organize your prayer requests to Adore God in Prayer:

Daily Prayer Requests   **Weekly Prayer Requests**

Sunday:

Monday:

Tuesday:

Wednesday:

Thursday:

Friday:

Saturday:

8. Ask God for a verse and a word for the year. For example, you might choose Proverbs 3:5, "Trust in the LORD with all your heart and do not lean on your own understanding." Your word for the year might be "trust." Focus on your verse and word throughout the year, attentive to all that God teaches you.

Year:

Verse:

Word:

NOTES

Week One, Day 1

1. The Barna Group, "The Bible," www.barna.org/FlexPage.aspx?Page=topic+topicID=7.

Week One, Day 2

1. J.I. Packer, *Knowing God* (Downers Grove, IL: InterVarsity Press © 1973), p 33. Used by permission.

2. Reprinted from *The Pursuit of God* by A.W. Tozer, copyright © 1982, 1993 by Christian Publications, Inc. Used by permission of Christian Publications, Inc., 800.233.4443, www.christianpublications.com.

Week One, Day 4

1. Used by permission from *A Place Apart* by Basil M. Pennington, copyright © 1998, Liguori Publications, Liguori, MO 63057, 1-800-325-9521.

2. Henri Nouwen, *The Way of the Heart* (New York: Ballantine Books, 1981), p. 17.

3. A.A. Bonar and R. McCheyne, *Memoirs and Remains of Robert Murray McCheyne* (Carlisle, PA: Banner of Truth Trust, 1996).

4. Henri Nouwen, "Moving from Solitude to Community to Ministry," *Leadership Journal*, Spring 1995, p. 81.

Week One, Day 6

1. Charles Haddon Spurgeon, *Morning and Evening* (New Kensington, PA: Whitaker House, 1997). See entry for December 27 PM.

Week Two, Day 7

1. John White, *Daring to Draw Near* (Downer's Grove, IL: InterVarsity Press, 1977), p. 100.

2. From *Toward Jerusalem* by Amy Carmichael, copyright © 1936 by the Dohnavur Fellowship. Published by CLC Publications, Fort Washington, PA 19034.

Week Two, Day 8

1. Quoted from *Spiritual Disciplines for the Christian Life* by Donald Whitney, copyright 1991. Used by permission of NavPress—http://www.navpress.com/. All rights reserved.

2. Reprinted from *The Pursuit of Man* by A.W. Tozer, copyright © 1950, 1978 by Lowell Tozer. Used by permission of Christian Publications, Inc., 800.233.4443. www.christianpublications.com.

3. A.A. Bonar and R. McCheyne, *Memoirs and Remains of Robert Murray McCheyne* (Carlisle, PA: Banner of Truth Trust, 1996), p. 4.

Week Two, Day 9

1. Henri Nouwen, *The Inner Voice of Love* (New York: Doubleday, 1996), p. xiii.

2. Ibid., p. xvi.

3. Ethel Marbach, "Maggie's Journal," quoted in Anne Broyles, *Journaling: A Spirit Journey* (Nashville: The Upper Room, 1988), p. 11.

4. A.W. Tozer, *Keys to the Deeper Life* (Grand Rapids, MI: Zondervan, 1988), pp. 28-29.

5. Anne Broyles, *Journaling: A Spirit Journey* (Nashville: The Upper Room, 1988), p. 12-13.

Week Two, Day 11

1. J.I. Packer, *Knowing God* (Downers Grove, IL: InterVarsity Press, 1975), pp. 18-19.

2. Reprinted from *The Pursuit of God* by A.W. Tozer, copyright © 1982, 1993 by Christian Publications, Inc. Used by permission of Christian Publications, Inc., 800.233.4443, www.christianpublications.com.

Week Two, Day 12

1. A.A. Bonar and R. McCheyne, *Memoirs and Remains of Robert Murray McCheyne* (Carlisle, PA: Banner of Truth Trust, 1996).

2. Charles Haddon Spurgeon, *Morning and Evening* (New Kensington, PA: Whitaker House, 1997). See entry for October 12 AM.

Week Three, Day 15

1. Merrill C. Tenney, *Galatians: The Charter of Christian Liberty* (Grand Rapids, MI: Wm. B. Eerdmans Publishing Company, 1960) pp. 207-08.

2. Dallas Willard, *Hearing God* (Downers Grove, IL: InterVarsity Press, 1984), p. 36.

Week Three, Day 18

1. Andrew Murray, *Abide in Christ* (Fort Washington, PA: Christian Literature Crusade, 1997), pp. 155-56.

2. F.S. Schenk, *The Bible Reader's Guide* (New York: American Tract Society, 1896), from the Introduction, "How to Study the Bible" by D.L. Moody.

Week Four, Day 19

1. Spiros Zodhiates, ed., *The Complete Word Study New Testament* (Chattanooga, TN: AMG Publishers, 1992), p. 941.

2. Ibid., p. 933.

3. Ibid., pp. 933-34.

4. Paul Lee Tan, ed., *Encyclopedia of 7700 Illustrations* (Rockville, MD: Assurance Publishers, 1979), p. 1458.

Week Four, Day 20

1. Fritz Reinecker and Cleon Rogers, *Linguistic Key to the Greek New Testament* (Grand Rapids, MI: Zondervan Publishing House, 1976), p. 549.

2. Ibid., p. 362.

Week Four, Day 21

1. Oswald Chambers, *My Utmost for His Highest* (Oswald Chambers Publications Assn., Ltd., 1963). See March 8 and December 9 entries.

Week Four, Day 22

1. *Man of Prayer,* © 1990, Frank Laubach, ProLiteracy Worldwide. Used by permission.

2. Emilie Griffin, *Wilderness Time* (San Fancisco: HarperSanFrancisco, 1989), p. 7.

Week Four, Day 23

1. Arthur Bennett, *The Valley of Vision* (Carlisle, PA: Banner Of Truth Trust, 2003).

Week Four, Day 24

1. Charles Haddon Spurgeon, *Morning and Evening* (New Kensington, PA: Whitaker House, 1997). See entry for February 19 AM.

Week Five, Day 26

1. A.W. Tozer, *The Knowledge of the Holy* (San Francisco: HarperSanFrancisco, 1978).

2. Fritz Reinecker and Cleon Rogers, *Linguistic Key to the Greek New Testament* (Grand Rapids, MI: Zondervan Publishing House, 1976), p. 605.

Week Five, Day 29

1. Brennan Manning, *The Signature of Jesus* (Sisters, OR: Questar Publishers, 1996), pp. 31-32. Used by permission of the author.

Week Five, Day 30

1. Charles Haddon Spurgeon, *Morning and Evening* (New Kensington, PA: Whitaker House, 1997). See entry for August 4 AM.

ACKNOWLEDGMENTS

Thank you, first of all, to my beloved husband, David Martin, MD, who has been my companion for almost half my life. Thank you, David, for helping me edit this book, for giving me wisdom in every aspect of this project, and for pushing me beyond my own limits. Thank you for being the love of my life.

Thank you to my mother, Elizabeth Snyder, for being my dearest friend and comrade throughout life. Thank you, dear Mother, for encouraging me to give my best and making me think I could dare mighty things in the name of the Lord. And then, thank you to my dad, Robert Snyder, for loving me and encouraging me in fair weather and in the storms of life. I love calling you on the phone to share the latest computer gizmo with you. And then to Rob and Tania, thank you for your love and for your encouragement, especially in this last year. Rob, you're the greatest brother a girl could ever have. Tania, what a blessing you are to me. And then, to my little Kayla, you are a bright shining star in my life, and when you are old enough, I expect you to travel with me when I speak and run my book table. Christopher, I love walking in the room and giving you a big hug and hearing about the latest sports activity. You have the greatest smile. Thank you to my mother-in-law, Eloise Martin, for praying for me and encouraging me these 20 years. You are my dear friend. Andy and Ann, Keegan and James, I thank God for you in my life. To my Nana, Mildred Snyder, thank you for being strong and sharp and for loving me.

Thank you, my dear friends, for launching out on this great adventure of knowing God. The Lord knew so well what it would mean to me to have friends who love Him and push me to know Him more. Andy Kotner, thank you for being my friend of friends and giving me such words of comfort in my hours of need. Conni Hudson, thank you for being a true friend, for saying "go for it" with every idea that I bring to the table, and for sharing my heart. Bev Trupp, thank you for cheering me on, listening to all my ideas, and for being such an example to me. Cindy Clark, thank you for always thinking outside the box, for your tireless service in Quiet Time Ministries, especially at my speaking engagements, and for loving to do the crazy, unusual thing (just like me!). Shirley Peters, thank you for loving the Lord and the Word of God the way you do. Your love for Him challenges me to remain steadfast and run my race well. Stefanie Kelly, thank you for using the gifts God has given you, for writing the most amazing music, and for ministering to my heart in amazing ways. Thank you especially for the song you wrote for me, "Seems like Days." I'll never forget the day you sang it to me (and all the women in our ministry). Thank you to Johnny Mann for writing the song "Quiet Time." I'll never forget sitting on your piano bench and sharing that moment of hearing it for the first time. Thank you to Paula U'Ren for sharing the beginning dreams of Quiet Time Ministries with me so many years ago. Thank you, Kelly Abeyratne, for praying to the Father on my behalf. Much has happened in my life and ministry because you have prayed.

Thank you to the Quiet Time Ministries staff team: Kayla Branscum (my assistant), Myra Murphy, Conni Hudson, Shirley Peters, Betty Mann, Cindy Clark, Kathleen Otremba, Jodi Adams, Sandi Rogers, Shelley Smith, Julie Airis, and Paula Zillmer. Thank you for meeting weekly for prayer for this ministry. To God be the glory!

A special thank-you to my two assistants—what a joy to serve the Lord with you! Kayla, what in the world would I do without you! I think you are amazing and so very gifted. Thank you for talking with people all over the United States and encouraging them in their quiet time. Thank you for the countless books you've printed, for the orders you've filled, for the speaking engagements you've organized, and for sharing my excitement about what God is doing in Quiet Time Ministries. Thank you for obtaining the permissions for this book and meticulously examining every detail. Shelley, thank you for being a servant of the Lord and doing so much for our women's ministries. Thank you for learning Photoshop and never being afraid to do anything.

Thank you to the *Enriching Your Quiet Time Magazine* staff and writers, Shirley Peters, Managing Editor, and Conni Hudson, Maurine Cromwell, and Cay Hough for exploring so many of the disciplines of devotion in your articles.

Thank you to the women at Southwest Community Church. You are my joy, and I so look forward to Thursday mornings when we can talk about God and His Word together. Thank you for your love and for putting together the most amazing surprises, especially for my birthday.

Thank you to the staff at Southwest Community Church for making ministry so fun. Thank you to Pastor Bob Thune for your commitment to studying, teaching, and preaching the Word of God. A special thanks to the Adult Ministries staff team, Pastor Rick Bailard, Pastor Jim Smoke, Shawna Koon, Shelley Smith, Debbie Sowles, Peggy Jackson, Pablo Cachon, and Lindsey and Kirk Miller.

Thank you to those who piloted *Six Secrets to a Powerful Quiet Time* and helped with so many wise suggestions: Jodi Adams, Julie Airis, Kayla Branscum, Melissa Brown, Cindy Clark, Georgeann DeWoody, Norma Greenleaf, Sharon Hastings, Betty Mann, Myra Murphy, Kathleen Otremba, Shelley Smith, Connie Sparks, Sherylen Yoak, and Paula Zillmer.

A special thank you to Jodi Adams of Jodi Adams Design who has helped at great length with all the graphics for Quiet Time Ministries. Thank you, Jodi, for sharing my love of design and typography. Thank you for sharing my dream for this book and helping with its style.

Thank you to Becky Freeman for your help in editing this book. Thank you to Betty Mann, Conni Hudson, and Shirley Peters for examining every passage of Scripture quoted in *Six Secrets to a Powerful Quiet Time,* ensuring its accuracy.

A special thank you also to Jim Smoke, author and minister, who has encouraged me to do what God has called me to do. Thank you, Jim, for knocking on my door when you first came here to church and for teaching me so many important principles of ministry.

Thank you to Greg Johnson of WordServe Literary Group for encouraging me in every aspect of my ministry. I'll never forget the day you came to the Quiet Time Ministries Resource and Training Center. It was a moment etched in time for me, and I'm so glad that we have the privilege of serving the Lord together. Thank you for representing me as my agent.

Thank you, Bob Hawkins Sr. for that exciting day when you met me in that bookstore, took chapters of this book, and sent them on to Harvest House. Your vision and passion for publishing is contagious. Thank you, Shirley Hawkins, for your kind words to me that day at the women's luncheon. Thank you, Bob Hawkins Jr. for your encouraging words and your vision for this book. And then, Terry Glaspey, thank you for having such a heart for the Lord and for all your encouragement to take this book to the world. Carolyn McCready, thank you for serving the Lord with excellence. It was a blessing to meet with you. Gene Skinner, thank you for your great attention to detail in editing. And finally, thank you to all the Harvest House team. I have been blessed.

Thank you to Vonette Bright for your special encouragement to me in Quiet Time Ministries. You are such an example to me, and I thank God for you. Thank you to Josh and Dottie McDowell for your example to me of how to serve the Lord in ministry. I will always be grateful for the time I spent on your ministry team and for your love and support through the years. Thank you Brenda Josee for teaching me so much about publishing. Your friendship has been a blessing "for such a time as this."

Thank you to Leann Pruitt McGee for teaching me how to have a quiet time so many years ago when I was involved in Campus Crusade for Christ at Arizona State University. Thank you to Kathy Cottrell and Helen Sommerfeld for being my special friends during that time and sharing my love for the Lord.

Thank you to all those who lead groups with the books of quiet times from Quiet Time Ministries across the nation and throughout the world. Oh, how we need leaders who will passionately love the Lord and teach His Word to others. I thank God for you and your commitment to give others the life-changing gift of a quiet time. Eternity will tell the amazing things that have happened because you said yes to the Lord and led your groups.

Thank you to the Board of Directors of Quiet Time Ministries: David Martin, Conni Hudson, Shirley Peters, and Jane Lyons, for faithfully encouraging and supporting this ministry. Thank you to all the prayer partners of Quiet Time Ministries. Eternity will reveal all that your prayers have accomplished for the kingdom of God. Thank you to those who give financially to this ministry. I could never have done any of this alone—your gifts have enabled us to launch out in Quiet Time Ministries.

ABOUT THE AUTHOR

Catherine Martin is a summa cum laude graduate of Bethel Theological Seminary with a Master of Arts Degree in Theological Studies. She is Founder and President of Quiet Time Ministries, Director of Women's Ministries at Southwest Community Church in Indian Wells, California, and on the adjunct faculty of Biola University. She is the author of *Six Secrets to a Powerful Quiet Time* published by Harvest House Publishers and *Pilgrimage of the Heart, Revive My Heart!,* and *A Heart That Dances* published by NavPress. She has also written *The Quiet Time Notebook, A Heart On Fire, A Heart to See Forever,* and The Quiet Time Classic Collection published by Quiet Time Ministries Press. She is Senior Editor for *Enriching Your Quiet Time* quarterly magazine and webmaster for Quiet Time Ministries Online at www.quiettime.org. As a popular speaker at retreats and conferences, Catherine challenges others to seek God and love Him with all of one's heart, soul, mind, and strength.

ABOUT QUIET TIME MINISTRIES

Quiet Time Ministries is a 501(c)3 publicly supported California nonprofit religious corporation with federal tax exempt status. Quiet Time Ministries offers resources for your quiet time including *The Quiet Time Notebook, Six Secrets to a Powerful Quiet Time* book, journal, and DVD, the Quiet Times for the Heart Series, *Pilgrimage of the Heart, Revive My Heart!, A Heart That Dances, A Heart on Fire,* the *Enriching Your Quiet Time* quarterly magazine, The Quiet Time Classic Collection, audios/videos/DVDs, and Quiet Time Ministries Online at www.quiettime.org. The Quiet Time Ministries Resources and Training Center located in Bermuda Dunes, California, offers conferences and workshops to encourage others in their relationship with the Lord.

Quiet Time Ministries
Post Office Box 14007
Palm Desert, CA 92255
1-800-925-6458
760-772-2357
www.quiettime.org

Other *Six Secrets to a Powerful Quiet Time* Resources
available from Quiet Time Ministries

www.quiettime.org
1-800-925-6458
760-772-2357

The *Six Secrets to a Powerful Quiet Time DVD* will enrich your individual or group experience with six companion video messages by Catherine Martin. Titles include "The One Thing in Life," "Find a Quiet Place," "Prepare Your Heart," "Set My Heart on Fire," "Seeking the Face of God," and "Will You Dance With Him?"

The *Six Secrets to a Powerful Quiet Time Journal* includes journal and prayer pages from *The Quiet Time Notebook.* This companion Journal offers space for writing, response, and prayers as you travel on your 30-day journey.